No Regrets

a novel

by Jo O'Connor

Michelle,
Wishing you
health, happiness
and peace

Jo O'Connor

First Edition – January 2013

ISBN-13: 978-1480275775
ISBN-10: 1480275778

Contents

Chapter 1 - Memories

"No regrets, no regrets, I have no regrets…" Those words were repeating over and over again in her mind as she drove down the deserted country road, past the Ridge towards Overlook. She was sorry she hadn't tried harder to get out of going to the Game.

At the moment it seemed like only a few weeks ago that he had stepped into her life and was prepared to cover her with his unblemished reputation, and protect her with a lifelong lie. Hot silent tears ran down her face as she gripped the steering wheel harder. The memory of his last words to her continued unabated, as the tightness in her chest grew.

There was no traffic on that winding road. The trees on both sides of the road and on the Ridge were bathed in bright sunlight. Their dying leaves were ablaze in the rustic colors of autumn. Yet, the day's golden splendor went unnoticed by Jane.

Too soon, she arrived at the rival high school. Her memories of the years gone by were seeking her undivided attention. Giving in to her memories was something Jane desired. To forget today and live in her yesterdays would have suited Jane. But others demanded her presence, and they kept her from living in her yesterdays.

Jane began walking towards the empty bleachers, her head bowed. She hoped that her early arrival would at least give her time to indulge in some of her treasured memories. As she settled down on the bottom bench of the nearest bleacher, Jane's mind quickly traveled back through the years to the day she met him.

She had just reached the main entrance to the cafeteria that Sunday evening May 4, 1958 when she heard her page. "Aha," she sighed as she picked up the wall phone just outside the doorway. "Hello, this is Dr. Potts."

"Dr. Potts, there is someone here to see you. Can you come right now?" Jane glanced around the empty cafeteria and said to the operator, "I'll be right up. Thank you."

"One of these days I'm going to eat meals on time with no interruptions," she grumbled under her breath as she left the cafeteria area and mounted the stairs to the main floor.

"Hi, Hazel!" Though tired and hungry, Jane flashed her ready smile at the busy switchboard operator and asked, "Someone looking for me?" Hazel pointed with her pencil at the back of a somewhat stout, yet tall, white-haired man, standing in the alcove across from the glassed-in switchboard area. Jane waved a thank you to the busy operator as she turned away and crossed the hall.

"Hello," she spoke in her soft, quiet voice. "You wanted to see me?" The tall man turned around at the sound of her voice.

"Jane Potts…Dr. Jane Potts?" He asked, even though he recognized her from her photograph.

"Yes," she answered with a questioning look.

"I'm Benjamin Franklin Bradley, Chairman of the Review Board at Switzer General Hospital." His smile was arresting. He had caught her off guard. As it had then, Jane's heart fluttered as she looked at Ben down the corridor of her memories.

"Oh, Doctor Bradley," she sounded surprised as she remembered to extend her hand. "I appreciate you're coming all the way here…but I didn't expect you today." She was aware she was sounding like a flustered school girl, failing to sound coherent and professional to the man who could help or harm her future.

"I had an opportunity to change my schedule so I was able to come earlier," he said as he took her small hand in his. Despite the smallness of her hand, he noticed her grip was firm and sure. "Hope my early arrival doesn't throw you a loop." He added, "I've never had a chance to visit the Windy City, thought I'd take the opportunity to do so."

"Oh no, it's just that this is my last week in the Emergency Room and who knows what the ER will be like this week. So I don't know if I'll have the time to answer your questions without interruptions," she bumbled, forgetting his mention of touring Chicago.

Again Bradley smiled his disarming smile in hopes of putting the obviously nervous intern at ease. "Don't worry; we'll find the time."

At that moment Jane was lost for more words. Her aching, empty stomach had her attention. "Umm Dr. Bradley, are you hungry?"

"As a matter of fact I could eat something. The meals on the plane are quite small…"

"Oh good," she interrupted. "I'm starved, I haven't had lunch yet and…" glancing at her watch, "the cafeteria will be closed in about fifteen minutes," she hurriedly added as she took his arm without another word and attempted to pull him in the direction of the elevator.

Gently but firmly he took her hand off his arm and assured her he could keep up with her. Once in the elevator, Jane pushed the basement button and breathed a sigh. "You haven't had lunch yet?" Bradley asked as he checked his watch. "It's past suppertime."

"I know, but it's been busy all day, busier than usual for a Sunday. I had a couple of pieces of toast this morning and gallons of coffee all day. But the coffee isn't sustaining me anymore."

"I'm not surprised, coffee has its limitations."

"Sure does," she agreed. When the elevator stopped, Jane leaped out followed by Bradley.

Inside the cafeteria area Jane noticed all the chalkboards announcing the meals of the day were blank. Forgetting she was not alone, she exclaimed, "Oh, for crying out loud!" Grabbing a tray she moved quickly along, looking disappointedly at each of the empty food containers. Sighing loudly, she came to the glass display case where three abandoned sandwiches waited. "Oh shoot,

7

sandwiches again, Yuk!!!" Jane stood staring at the three sandwiches, seemingly mesmerized. Forgotten, standing beside her, Bradley quietly observed her.

Suddenly from behind the display case a plump, pleasant-looking woman called out, "Are you trying to decide which sandwich you want or memorizing what they look like, Dr. Potts?"

Jane snapped out of her trance-like pose and asked, "Maxine, isn't there anything besides these sandwiches?"

"No, so choose now or move aside and let that gentleman pass you," Maxine said as she nodded and smiled at Bradley.

"Dr. Bradley is with me, Maxine." Jane leaned closer to the glass case and pointed. "Maxine, I think rigor mortis has set in on those sandwiches. How long have they been here?"

"They were made this morning, so none of your bad mouthing about the food, Dr. Potts. The sandwiches are fine. Which one do you want?"

Jane answered, "I think I'll pass on those lifeless sandwiches, Maxine. I really wanted something hot for dinner. Don't you have anything hot, like soup maybe?"

"No, sorry. Why didn't you come here earlier, like everybody else did?"

"Because I was busy in the Emergency Room."

"All the other ER people managed to come in while we were serving hot meals today. So you could have."

"If I could have gotten away I would have," Jane insisted.

Remembering she was not alone in the lunch line, Jane turned to her visitor. "Oh, I'm sorry, Dr. Bradley. What sandwich do you want?" Jane asked

"It doesn't matter; pick what you want."

Looking exasperated and straight at Jane, Maxine said, "I tell you what, you take these three sandwiches and I'll throw in a couple of pickles."

8

"You have a bargain, we'll do that." Bradley spoke up to the surprise of both women as he took the three sandwiches and put them on Jane's tray.

"I'll be right back with the pickles," Maxine promised.

In the meantime Jane moved further down the line and grabbed two small bottles of chocolate milk out of the refrigerator case. "Want chocolate milk, Dr. Bradley?"

"Ah, no thanks," Bradley said as he reached for a coffee cup and started to lift the handle on the coffee urn.

"That's gut rot by now, I wouldn't drink it," Jane warned.

"Oh?" he exclaimed as he let go of the lever and put the coffee cup down.

"Do you want some juice? There are some soft drinks too."

"I'll take a look." He moved behind her to the refrigerated cabinet.

"Here are your pickles."

"Thank you Maxine." Jane took the plate being handed her. Sniffing the air she asked, "Maxine, is that turkey roasting?"

"It is," Maxine answered and motioned with her hands to move along.

"When's it going to be ready?"

"Later tonight, it's for a private party."

"What party?"

"That's none of your business, Dr. Potts! Now move along. I'm going to close the cafeteria in ten minutes so you need to eat and be out of here in ten minutes."

"Now wait a minute Maxine, who is the party for? Maybe we can get invited to it and have some turkey."

"That's not going to happen on both accounts. Now move along, Dr. Potts."

"Ah come on tell me who is the party for and I'll ask for an invite. I'm so sick of sandwiches," she pleaded. "And," she added, " I'll even stop bad-mouthing the food

9

here… even though none of the stuff you guys put out would win a blue ribbon in a county fair!"

"Who do you know that wins blue ribbons for cooking?"

"My mother does, with everything she cooks for the county fair!"

"How nice for you! Sorry Doc, you have to be here during operating hours or else you get what's left over and those sandwiches are all that's left," Maxine said with finality.

"I believe the lady means what she says, Dr. Potts, so why don't we just take these sandwiches and move on."

Maxine looked at Bradley and nodded a thank-you.

"All right Maxine, we'll get out of your way! Have a nice time at the party tonight!" Jane stated in a flippant tone.

"I'm sure I will and I will be thinking of you, Dr. Potts," Maxine grinned and responded in an equally flippant tone.

Bradley and Jane settled at one of the empty tables. Jane pushed all three sandwiches towards Bradley. "You pick first, Dr. Bradley. I really am sick of sandwiches. Besides I love chocolate milk and I can survive on that!"

Just as Jane was about to uncap one of them, a familiar page resounded in the empty cafeteria.

"Oh for heaven's sake!" she exclaimed. "Someone doesn't like me! Excuse me, Dr. Bradley. I have to answer that."

Bradley stood up as she got up. "I'll be here," he said, and then sat down as Jane headed straight to the nearest house phone. His eyes remained on her as she answered the page. He was thinking he had not made a mistake in coming to Chicago to meet with this candidate. It was true he had not had the opportunity to visit the famous Windy City, but the real reason he had come, he decided to keep to himself, at least for a while.

Minutes later she was back at the table looking pleased. "I have to take care of some paper work and after that I can leave. I've been here since 6 this morning, so I'll..."

He interrupted, "Is there a place to eat in walking distance?"

"Yes, there is an all-night diner just a block up the street. I've eaten there a few times. The food is good and reasonably priced."

"Tell you what, why don't we go there as soon as you finish your paper work?"

"Really, you want to do that, Dr. Bradley? That would be great!"

Her excitement at the prospect of eating at the diner amused Bradley. "Fine then, the sooner you do your paper work the sooner we can have a hot meal, " he added as he took her arm and left the uneaten sandwiches and pickles behind.

They had taken a few steps when she stopped and said, "Wait! My chocolate milk!" Turning, she grabbed the two small bottles and stuffed them in the pockets of her lab coat. All the while Bradley kept a firm grip on her arm.

Back in the ER, Jane quickly introduced Bradley to the staff, then found a chair and empty writing space and began filling out the additional paper work.

Later that evening Dr. Bradley and Dr. Potts sat in the cozy diner chatting amicably. Having finished their hot meal, Bradley asked, "Dessert?"

"Oh no I can't eat one more thing, I feel so much better, I'm so glad you suggested this, thank you."

"You're welcome, Dr. Potts," Bradley said as he took the bill out of her hands. "Let me take care of this."

"Oh no that's all right I can pay for mine Dr. Bradley. And by the way you can call me Jane if you like, outside the hospital." She smiled.

"I was an intern once, Jane, and I know how little money interns have so let me take care of this." His tone of voice left no more room for argument. Jane nodded her thanks.

Outside the spring winds were like a gentle breeze, so unusual, yet so pleasant as the two walked arm-in-arm back towards the hospital.

"You know Dr. Bradley, I bet I could stand in one place and fall asleep like a horse, right now."

"I believe that. Life as an intern can be exhausting."

"And yet, I'd like to sit somewhere and chat more with you. But I really, really need to get some sleep, and besides I don't want to do anything that would make Mrs. Bradley question my motives. That just wouldn't be smart," she beamed.

"I am a widower, Jane, have been for more than ten years."

"Oh, I am sorry, Dr. Bradley," she said with sincerity.

"Thank you," he said.

Wanting to change the subject, she asked, "Can I ask you a question you've probably been asked a million times?"

"Would that be, am I a descendant of The Benjamin Franklin?"

"Yup, that's the question!"

"Yes I am, he is my great-grandfather ten times removed, on my mother's side."

"Wow that's exciting; my brother would be thrilled to meet you."

"Why is that?"

"Because he has a doctorate in Western Civilization, and a master's degree in American History. He loves to expound on the personality and character of the founding fathers. So he would be thrilled to know about you, and being the polite gentleman farmer and professor that he is, he'd probably ask if he could send you some questions about your grandfather."

Bradley smiled. "I'd be happy to answer his questions, if I can."

12

Unknowingly, Bradley had begun to endear himself to Jane with that one offer to cooperate with her brother.

Jane glanced at her watch; it was almost ten. She sighed, "Honestly, Dr. Bradley, I could sit and chat with you all night long, but I have to get some sleep. I'm back on at six tomorrow morning."

"You can call me Benjamin, Jane, except when we're in the hospital," he grinned. "Where's your dorm?"

"It's on the hospital grounds."

"I'll walk you there and then I think I'll turn in."

"Are you sure you want to walk me to my dorm? I think you'll have to walk another couple of blocks to get to your hotel."

"I'm sure," he said while he was picturing his hotel room with its two double beds and wishing he could invite the young intern to sleep in one of those beds.

By late Tuesday afternoon Bradley had concluded his interview with Jane and had spoken to some instructors, other doctors and charge nurses and all who had written references for Jane Potts. He had also reviewed her outstanding academic records, again. And before Wednesday morning had slipped into afternoon he had written his own recommendation based on his interviews and mailed a mimeographed copy of it off to his office in Glenwood.

That evening Benjamin was already thinking in terms of a future that included Jane in an intimate way. He had also come to realize Jane was unassuming and socially naive.

Bradley managed to meet Jane for lunch every day during his stay and often after lunch he occupied himself with exploring Chicago, but in the evenings, he dedicated all of his time to Jane.

It was a balmy Friday evening when they walked slowly back from the diner and settled themselves on their favorite bench outside her dorm.

13

"Just for a little while, Benjamin...I am so tired, and I'll have to go in, I'm sorry," she said as she leaned her head against his chest and closed her eyes.

Ben's arms tightened around her as he bent his head and lightly kissed the top of her head. Looking at her he was reminded of his days as an intern and remembered again how exhaustion had been his closest companion.

Chapter 2 - Sunday

Saturday had moved along rather slowly; the ER had seen fewer patients than usual for a Saturday. By four that afternoon, Jane was able to close the door on her time in the Emergency Room. She hadn't seen or heard from Benjamin all day and wondered if he had left Chicago. Disappointed in not seeing him, Jane looked downcast as she walked slowly to her dorm.

She lay down on her bed and was just slipping into a light sleep when she heard her name being called. "Jane, Jane!"

"Yes," she answered in a tired voice.

"There is someone waiting for you upstairs in the sitting room."

"Are you coming?" the resident student nurse asked.

"Yes, I'm coming." Too tired to pin her hair up, Jane climbed the stairs yawning as she went. He stood up in the sitting room, smiling, as soon as she appeared. Though delighted to see him, Jane for some reason thought Benjamin looked as though he had a secret.

"I'm sorry Jane I haven't been around but I've been busy touring the city. I'm leaving tomorrow."

"Oh, when?" She asked in a flat emotionless tone, because she did not want him to suspect how much she would miss him.

"My flight leaves at seven thirty-five tomorrow night. Have you eaten? " he asked.

"Yes I have. Have you?"

"I'm not hungry. Want to go for a walk?"

"That would be nice," she said, "but let me go straighten myself up. I was about to take a nap."

"You look fine, Jane. Come on," He said as he took her arm and led her outside and over to one of the benches. Once they sat down he kissed her. "I've been thinking about kissing you all day. Sorry, I couldn't wait any longer."

15

Smiling, she said, "Don't apologize. I like your kisses, Dr. Benjamin Franklin Bradley. I thought you had gone back to New York. I'm glad you didn't."

"I wouldn't have left without first telling you."

"That's good to know." In the next breath she said "Oh, I have a nice surprise."

"What is it?"

"I have two free tickets to the Playhouse for tomorrow and I have all Sunday off. I love mysteries and the play is 'Ten Little Indians' by Agatha Christie. Would you like to go with me? It's a matinee and it starts at 2 p.m. I can drive us to the Playhouse and then afterwards I can take you to the airport." In her excitement Jane sounded almost breathless.

"You've got a date."

"Great!"

After the play and dinner Jane drove them to the airport. Bradley was talkative. "You know, Jane, I finished my inquiries on Tuesday and I spent the rest of this week getting to know you socially," he confessed.

"Did you, really?" She sounded surprised. "I thought you were observing how I interacted with staff and patients and out exploring Chicago. You know I appreciated your taking me to lunch and dinner, Dr. Bradley, but most of all I am going to miss your company." No sooner had she spoken her thoughts than she remembered the main reason Dr. Bradley had come to Chicago. "I hope I'm not sounding bold. I wouldn't want you to think what I'm saying is to persuade you to accept me on the residency program in your hospital, because that is not my intention…it would be like cheating and I don't believe in cheating. Besides the truth is I, I do like you, Doctor Bradley and I am glad you came." She rattled on in her nervous way.

"Socially, it's Benjamin or Ben." Bradley glanced at his watch as he reminded her for what seemed liked the

16

thousandth time that week. "We have about ten minutes before I have to check in. Will you be going in the terminal with me, Jane?"

"Of course, I wouldn't leave you to wait alone."

"Good, but I'll say my good byes here away from prying eyes." Again Jane looked surprised and wondered why he was concerned about prying eyes. Bradley slid close to her and pressed his lips over hers. His kiss left her feeling breathless and weak.

It took a few moments before she could speak and when she did, she asked, "Why did you kiss me like this now and not before?"

"Are you complaining, Jane?" He smiled as he released her.

"No, it's just that, well, it was wonderful!" she explained and adding with a grin, "You're a good kisser, Doc."

Ben beamed at the young face looking at him with a questioning smile.

"Jane, I wanted to kiss you like that the first night we went to dinner. Too many kisses like that and we would have both ended up stark naked somewhere behind some bushes making love. And I don't think either one of us want to be arrested for indecent exposure!"

Jane laughed, "You're right. But I must say you do know how to stir up the most intimate of feelings, with your kisses."

"I'm glad to hear I still can, Jane," he said in a serious tone, "because I haven't stirred any woman in about a dozen years."

Jane sounded surprised. "Really!"

"Naturally, when my wife was sick we had no relations and after she died I concentrated more on building my practice and that kept me quite busy and then I ended up with more responsibilities and even less time for myself when I accepted the hospital Administrator's position and later on I became committed to building an intern and residency program and I ended up becoming chairman of that as well so I've had no time for myself."

"But after reading your introductory letter and seeing your enclosed photograph I thought it would be wise to meet you for reasons beside your residency application. I haven't been disappointed," he added.

For a few moments neither spoke, Jane mulling over the idea of asking what he meant while Benjamin wondered if it had been smart to say anything about his other reason for coming. Instead, the two had separately decided not to speak on the subject of that unusual revelation. "I think we ought to go into the terminal now," Bradley suggested as he broke the silence between them.

Still puzzled, Jane smiled, "Yes, of course." He reached behind the bench seat and retrieved his luggage before heading into the airport.

As they walked towards the terminal Jane jokingly said, "Maybe I should start a taxi service to Midway. I was here the week before you came."

"Oh?" Benjamin responded in a mildly interested tone. "Who did you bring here?"

"My former boyfriend, we said goodbye for the last time. He was on his way to Germany."

"Is he in the military?" asked Bradley, now very interested.

"No, he's an architect. The company he works for does business nationally and internationally. I could see we were not right for each other about a month ago. So when I told him I would not go to Europe with him and do my residency there he was not happy but it did make breaking up easier."

"So the break up is for good?"

"Definitely, especially since I now realize I wasted almost a year of my love on him," she added firmly.

Bradley had decided he wasn't interested in hearing details about her previous romantic involvement and subsequent break up so he made no comment. Instead, inside the terminal he immediately went to the ticket counter to check in.

At the boarding gate Bradley reached into his breast pocket and pulled out a card. "Jane, here is my card. I've written my home phone number on the back for you. If you need something or just want to talk you can call my home telephone, collect. All right?"

"Yes, thank you." Jane looked down at his card trying to decide if it was a mistake telling him about Matt. She had come to like Bradley very much and now thought he might have lost interest in her.

A call to board had broken into her thoughts. She looked up at Bradley and saw a pensive look on his face as he looked at her. She had a feeling her relationship with Bradley would now be on a professional level. He was just being nice to her and that was how she had to think about him, she told herself.

"I guess I'd better board now," he said adding, "I'll let you know about your next interview."

He was about to turn and go when she said, "Thank you for coming and for everything. I'll miss you, Benjamin."

He looked deeply into her eyes and saw a hint of sadness beginning to surface and said "You are welcome, Jane; I've enjoyed being with you." Then he turned away and headed to the open door without another word.

She moved closer to the window that made up most of the wall facing the tarmac. It was already lined with people waving goodbye. She watched to see if he would turn and wave to her. He did not.

Still, she stayed watching until the plane headed towards the runway. In silence she reminded herself he would always be on a professional level with her and wondered if New York State was the place to do her residency.

It was like the day she brought Matt Hunter to this same airport; she had a deep sense of loss despite her resolution

19

to break up with him. So, now it was the same feeling as she drove onto the highway leading away from Midway Airport, only this time tears began to slip down her face. She was wondering how could she have such deep feelings for a man almost fifteen years her senior and whom she had known for no more than a week. But as she drove she realized the feelings were real and why and how they had come upon her so quickly she didn't understand.

But in any case there was nothing more she could say to Benjamin Franklin Bradley. She did believe he didn't like hearing about Matt and guessed she would not be hearing from Benjamin again. She decided not to call him, for any reason.

In her room she settled down to thumb through the week's worth of mail she had ignored. There were letters from some of the other hospitals where she had applied to their pediatrics residencies program. At first she thought they were a godsend, but they held her attention only for a moment, then she set them aside.

Chapter 3 - A Beginning

It was long after eleven that night when she awoke to a loud knock on her door and a woman's voice calling out. "Jane, are you up?"

"Yes," Jane answered in a sleepy voice.

"There's a long distance telephone call for you upstairs."

"I'll be right there, thank you." Jane had fallen asleep in the chair and it took a minute or two for her to get up and get moving. A long distance call at this hour couldn't be good news she thought as she made her way upstairs to the large sitting room where the housemother's desk sat with its private phone. Mrs. Homes eyed Jane as she entered the room.

"I'll be in the kitchen, Jane, if you need me."

"Thank you, Mrs. Homes." Jane waited until she heard the housemother's footsteps fade down the hallway before picking up the telephone handset.

"This is a person-to-person call for Dr. Jane Potts."

"Yes, that's me, operator, thank you."

"You're welcome."

"Your call, sir."

"Thank you operator" and in the same breath he asked, "Jane?"

"Yes," she answered, still trying to wake up.

"Did I wake you?"

"Yes, but that's ok uh…"

"Jane, it's me, Ben." He was aware she was a little uncertain who was on the other end of the call.

"Oh, you're home already?"

"Yes, got home a few minutes ago. All I could think about on the flight was you, Jane

"I'm going to see if the Board can meet Tuesday and do a last review of the resident's applications for pediatrics and set up interview schedules."

"Please don't make any final decision on your residency, Jane. I know they want you to stay there in Chicago, but Jane, I want you close to me. I can't promise you a residency here, but I can try to get you a residency in a hospital near me. Just let me try, Jane. Remember I only have a tiebreaker vote on the board but I will emphasize your qualifications. I think the Board will vote for you because of your academic achievements and your strong recommendations, but just in case please don't make any promises to any other hospitals."

"Well, it will depend, but I guess I can wait…" She sounded unsure, wondering if she could really wait long before making a decision.

He cut short what else she was going to say…"You sound as though you are still half asleep so I'll hang up. Just one more thing, can I call you tomorrow night?"

"Um, tomorrow's Monday, right?"

"Yes." She could hear him chuckle over her temporary uncertainty. "Ok, one more minute, will you be in your room tomorrow night?"

"Yes, but I don't have a phone."

"I know, Jane; look, can you call me say around seven, collect on my home number, instead?"

"Probably"

"Ok, I'll expect your call at my home tomorrow at seven. Hopefully I'll be able to let you know if the Board will meet on Tuesday. If I'm not there, try again."

"Okay."

"Go back to sleep, Jane. Good night."

"Good night, and thanks for calling." When Jane heard the click of the receiver on the other end, then she hung up.

That Monday as Jane moved from patient to patient her footsteps seemed lighter than usual. She felt less tired and more energetic. Jane attributed all of this to his calling last night. She really hadn't expected the call, and she kept reminding herself of his statement that he wanted her to be near him. She asked herself again could it possibly be true, that she had fallen in love with Benjamin Franklin Bradley, and he with her? She needed to think about that during a time when she wasn't going from door to door seeing patients. It was important to concentrate on the patients. That was her primary objective, she reminded herself. She had worked too hard and sacrificed so much for too long, to make any blunders now, and jeopardize her future in medicine.

Jane was just leaving her last patient of the morning and heading down to the cafeteria when she heard her page. Stepping up her pace, she flew down the rest of the stairs and into the wide-open hallway just outside of the cafeteria. As she reached for the nearest wall phone she was thinking how glad she was that she had finished her time as intern in the emergency room last week. But, it was a shame that Benjamin had not come this week; it would have been easier to have more time with him while she was on the Med Service floor.

"Hello, this is Dr. Potts, you paged me?'

"Yes," the voice at the other end replied "You have a long distant call would you like me to put it through to you where you are?"

Jane caught her breath before answering. "Yes, thank you."

Jane heard the switchboard operator tell the caller. "Doctor Potts is on the line now." And with that she heard "Jane?"

"Yes…Dad, is that you?" she asked in a worried tone. "Is something wrong?"

"No Sis, we were just wondering when you were coming home. Are you going to have some time off before you start your residency?"

"I'll have about two weeks before I start, but that will depend on where I'll be doing my residency."

Before she could explain her father questioned,. "I thought you were going to do your residency there?"

"I decided to apply to other hospitals to see what options I have before I make a final decision."

"That sounds like a good idea. Maybe you'll get something closer to home."

"Dad, is there something you want to tell me? Are you sure nothing is wrong?" she asked, still worried.

Jane heard her father sigh a long, deep impatient sigh. "No, there isn't anything wrong, Jane; it's just we had a long distance call a few minutes ago from Germany…"

"Germany!" Jane exclaimed before her father could finish.

"Let me finish! Matt Hunter called."

"What did he want?" she asked impatiently

"Jane, stop interrupting me and I'll tell you. He wanted to know when you were coming home because he wanted to surprise you and be here when you arrived."

"Did you tell him he could not come, he wouldn't be welcomed?"

"Jane, wait until I finish please! I said we didn't know if or when you would be having time off, or if you would be home. I mentioned we had only seen you a few days over the last two years, and if you have some time we would like to have you spend it with us. I think he got the hint, Jane. He is an intelligent young man."

"So, where else have you applied?" Her father asked as he considered the former subject closed.

"Dad, I do not want him to know where I go to do my residency, or when I come home. I'd rather wait to let you know if I've been accepted first."

"You know we aren't going to say anything."

"I know, it's just I want to be accepted first before I say where I'm going."

"Jane," her father's voice revealed a deep concern. "Are you afraid of Matt, do you think he would harm you?"

"No, Dad, not at all." she answered quietly. "Did he tell you we had broken up?"

"He just said you two had a difference of opinion, and he wanted to patch things up."

"Dad, I really don't think I want to see him again. Please don't let Matt try to put you in the middle of things, just say you don't know to any of his questions. I really think that would be best." Scott Potts agreed.

Jane deliberately left out telling her father about Benjamin Franklin Bradley.

Chapter 4 - To Understand

Dr. Bradley's very clear instructions were included with the prepaid round trip airline tickets that had arrived. Jane was to be in New York on the afternoon of the last Wednesday in May. Her interview would be at one in the afternoon the following day, Thursday, May 29, 1958. In the mean time, Jane took her board certification exam as a general practitioner, in Illinois.

Jane had been a bit anxious about flying and had jokingly told Bradley she had been thinking of taking a Greyhound Bus instead. Bradley argued the trip to New York by plane would be much quicker, and that she needed to get used to flying. He didn't say why.

The night before her flight she had learned Bradley would not be meeting her at the airport, and that she was to take a cab to the hotel she was booked in through Friday. In her hotel room Jane took a quick look at the bed, kicked off her shoes, and stepped out of her dress, then slipped under the bed spread and was soon asleep.

It was early evening when there was what sounded like someone pounding on something. Her drowsy mind couldn't quite judge where the sounds were coming from. After a few seconds she remembered where she was and realized the pounding sounds were actually the knocking on her door. She threw off the bedspread and went to the door. Benjamin Franklin Bradley's face broke into a broad smile as he looked at the young woman standing in her slip and stockings.

Quickly, he stepped inside shut the door behind him and then took her into his arms and kissed her as he had done before.

It was that breath-taking kiss that left Jane weak like a rag doll in Bradley's arms. Moments later Jane recovered and repeated, "You're quite the kisser, Doc!"

"Thank you," he beamed. "I'm sorry I couldn't meet you at the airport. I had a number of patients to see this afternoon and some things I had to finish up before Friday."

"Have you had dinner yet?" he asked

"No, I was tired and fell asleep. What time is it?"

"It's almost five-thirty. How about getting dressed and we'll eat in the dining room downstairs?"

"Okay."

The dining room was impressive with its long windows and wide dark wood trim over the windows and doors. The white stucco walls and heavy dark furniture made for a good imitation of an old English pub.

While waiting for their dinner, Dr. Bradley began the conversation with, "I've arranged to take the whole month of June through the first week in July off. Everyone involved in covering for me agreed with me when I said I deserve some real time off. So that is settled."

"How long has it been since you took time off, Dr. Bradley?"

"It's Ben, remember?"

"Yes, sorry."

"It has been more than a decade since I took any time off."

"It has been a while for me too. I found out I have worked so much time for some of my classmates, plus some extra time, that yesterday was my last day as an intern."

"Really," he said sounding as though he was surprised, which he was not. "How..., convenient."

"Yes, it is. I am going to fly back to Chicago and then drive home during that time off. I have only been home for a couple of days since I started my internship and I missed out on going home for the Christmas Holidays, both years too."

Her proposed trip home took him by surprise. He quickly realized he needed to try and impress her with his trip and hopefully convince her to travel with him. He

27

began by saying, "My vacation will take me from the Desert to the Rockies to the Atlantic Ocean to Lake Ontario."

"Wow! Sounds like you're planning a trip to make up for lost time. Where, specifically?"

"First, I'm going to fly to Reno, Nevada, and spend a couple of days touring that area; then I'm going to drive to Yellowstone National Park, look around for a day or two, then on to the Grand Tetons. From the Tetons I'll head east to the Great Northern Maine woods and from there I'll head down to Cape Cod then back to New York and a few days fishing on Lake Ontario."

"Oh, nice!" Jane's dreamy eyes were picturing the trip. Forgive me, but I think I'm jealous, Doc."

Her statement was a spark of hope. "Would you like to go with me? I could easily include a stop in Indiana for a few days on the way to the Northern Maine woods." Bradley reached across the table and took her hand in his. "I missed you, Jane."

Jane smiled sweetly and took a deep breath and said,. "I missed you too, Ben. I really did. Even though I was able to talk to you on the phone, it wasn't the same as your being in Chicago." Looking serious, she began,. "Ben, I have to ask you, face to face now, did you really like the play?"

"I believe I've answered that at least three times already." He looked perplexed. She had completely ignored his invitation to go on vacation with him and he couldn't understand why she was still asking about the play.

"I know, but this time it's face to face. On the way to the airport I asked you and you just mumbled something I didn't catch, and I didn't think I should push. And on the phone you sort of tossed out a positive, and then I asked you again a few days later at the risk of sounding forgetful…"

"Why do you keep asking, did that play mean so much to you?"

"No, it's just, well, I wondered if it was something you would really like to do again? I really enjoy going to plays."

"Jane, do you like football games? Tell me truthfully."

"Not really, I don't know much about sports."

"Suppose I asked you to go to a football game with me or maybe a basketball game, would you go?"

"Yes, I would go."

"Why?"

"Because I like being with you, Ben."

"And that's the same reason I would go with you to more plays. Jane, you are very special to me." Benjamin's hand closed over her hand. Just then the waiter appeared and Benjamin ordered for them.

After they finished eating, Jane asked a question that had been troubling her ever since meeting Ben. "Ben, you wouldn't pull any strings for me so I can get into the resident program, would you?"

Ben leaned back in his chair, his hand tugged at his lower lip for a thoughtful moment. Then he said, "Jane, I have to separate my professional life from my personal life. I can't in good conscience pull any strings, even for you."

Jane looked relieved. "Thank you Ben, I don't want you to ever use your influence for me. I prefer the merit system. Which reminds me, I have to go to bed early tonight. My interview is tomorrow."

"How about first going on a drive? It's a beautiful night."

"All right, but not for a long drive."

It wasn't a long drive out in the country to Benjamin's house. On a post, a brightly lit electric lamp stood at attention at the beginning of a slate walkway that led to the front door.

"This is my home, Jane."

Inside his house Ben first led Jane to the kitchen. She noted it had numerous cabinets and every modern

29

appliance, every convenience, but it was somewhat bland. Though the table and four chairs did help make the room inviting.

"Can I make you some coffee?" he asked as she was looking closely at this modern kitchen.

"No, thank you, I need to sleep tonight so I won't sound too much like a blithering idiot during my interview."

"Well then, let me show you the rest of my house. I had it built to my specifications, so everything is pretty convenient."

Except for the stone fireplace on the front wall and the built-in bookcases filled with books lining two walls perpendicular to each other, there wasn't anything notable about the living room. The dining room had a large five-arm brass light fixture that hung over the center of a heavy-looking dark wood dining table. While both rooms were handsomely furnished, there was nothing warming about them. The walls were without photographs, paintings, anything decorative or sentimental.

The ell extension was the bedroom area. There were two doorways on one side of the hallway and three on the opposite side. Two roomy identical bedrooms were on one side with a small home office. In between the two bedrooms, on the opposite side, was the door to a full bathroom and beyond that door was another door that led to a large bedroom.

Ben led Jane into his bedroom. It was an unusually large room. There were two doors on one long wall. One door, Jane discovered, opened into a huge walk-in closet while the other opened up to a very modern bathroom.

"Wow, you have a bathroom in your bedroom!"

"It's called a master bath. The builder told me that in the future most new houses would include a bathroom in the master bedroom."

"It's very nice, Ben. That bed looks huge." she stated as her attention turned back into the bedroom and to his neatly made up bed. "It is; I had it made especially for me. I am

six foot five and I wanted a bed I could stretch out on
without hitting headboard or footboard."

Chapter 5 - To Celebrate

Friday, May 30, 1958 Jane was sitting on a wooden bench beneath a large fragrant lilac bush in full bloom, waiting. She was not sure how she had come across in the tough interview with the Board. One thing was certain; if she didn't shine in that interview she would not be given a second chance at Switzer General Hospital. All morning she had been going over in her mind the questions and her answers, trying to find an area in which she might have stumbled. She just wasn't sure.

It was a little after noon when Benjamin came out of the hospital with a letter in his hand. The board had voted. The acceptance and the rejection letters were written and signed. "Jane." Benjamin handed her the sealed envelope addressed to her. His face was expressionless.

"Thank you." Jane took the letter from him and opened it. She was unconsciously holding her breath as she read it. Jane's letter welcomed her to the Switzer General Hospital's Pediatric Residency program.

Her fate settled, she heaved a sigh of relief. "You didn't use your position to sway the Board in my favor?" she asked.

"No, Jane, I told you I couldn't do that in good conscience. You got in on your own." Benjamin reassured her.

Benjamin was standing behind her while she read her letter. He came around the bench and put out his hand. With a bright smile she shook his hand. "Congratulations, Jane."

"Thank you, Ben."

"Let's go, my car is right over here."

"Where are we going?"

"You'll see."

In Overlook, Benjamin parked near the hot dog stand. He got out and was back in his car in a matter of minutes with hot dogs for both of them, chocolate milk for Jane and a soft drink for himself.

After they finished their lunch he began. "Listen, Jane, let's celebrate tonight. There is a restaurant just outside of town here that serves great meals. And, they have a band and there's dancing. I think that's the place we should go to celebrate. What do you think?"

"It sounds very nice but I'm not a very good dancer."

"Don't worry, Jane, my dancing skills are rusty. We will just do our best and have some fun. We'll be fine,." he assured her.

Jane smiled, "All right."

"Good, do you have a dressy dress with you? It's a pretty formal place."

Benjamin did his best to describe the dress code for this special place. Her answer was no.

"There are a couple of nice department stores here. I'm sure you can find sales ladies that will help you. Just tell them that we're going to Van Durham's tonight. They will know what you should wear. Just remember, the more cleavage you show the greater the invitation,." he grinned.

"What do you mean by 'invitation'?"

"I'll explain later, I have to get back to the hospital. When you are finished, take a cab back to the hotel. There is a cab company office right on Main Street. I'll make our reservation for seven-thirty tonight, but I'll plan on picking you up at seven. Oh, and be sure you are all packed. Okay?"

"Okay," she promised.

Benjamin noticed her worried look when he suggested shopping. He was certain Jane didn't have much money for party dresses and whatever else ladies wear with special dresses. He reached into his wallet and handed her some money. "Just keep it in your wallet until you are ready to pay for your purchases."

"But this looks like a lot of money! Ben, I really can't take it,." she said as she held it out to him.

33

"Jane, just think of us going to a Ball and all you would wear to it. Maybe you'll want to get your hair done too. Look Jane, I haven't had anyone to go out with, or to buy anything for, in almost a dozen years, so take the money and have fun shopping for our date," he said as he pulled onto Main Street and into a parking space in downtown Overlook.

"But..."

"No buts, you've earned a special evening and besides I'm looking forward to the evening." Benjamin opened the door for her and then waved as he drove out of the parking space.

At exactly seven that evening there was a knock on Jane's hotel room door. "Well, Dr. Bradley, you look very handsome this evening," Jane smiled as she opened wide the door for Benjamin who was smartly dressed in a dark suit.

"Thank you, Dr. Potts." He took a long look at the attractively-dressed young woman and said, "You look beautiful." She was wearing a form-fitting black cocktail dress with a lacy shawl that covered the top half of her dress and was gathered together on her shoulder and held in place by a large sparkling brooch. Her long hair had been done up in curls and waves. At her ears she wore sparkling earrings. Her black satin high heels and black silk nylons completed her formal look.

"Are you ready to go? Have everything packed?" he asked in rapid succession.

"Yes, I am. Just let me get my suitcase and coat." She said as she turned away and moved towards her waiting suitcase.

"I'll get that," he said as he snapped up her suitcase before she could.

Inside the car Benjamin turned to face Jane. The hotel's outside lights were bright. "You look stunning, Jane." He said in a low husky voice as he gently encircled her with his arms and kissed her lightly on the lips.

"Thank you, Benjamin. I didn't want to disappoint you. I wanted to look especially nice for you."

"You haven't disappointed me Jane, thank you. Now, how about we head off to dinner and a dance?" He asked as he started up his car and headed towards the Van Durham in Overlook.

Inside the Van Durham the maitre d' stood at his podium and was checking off Dr. Bradley's name when he turned to get a better look at the doctor's date. His eyes expressed a look of approval to Dr. Bradley as he motioned the couple to follow him and handed them their menus once they were seated.

"Know what you want to eat?"

"Oh!" She breathed, as she looked at the menu.

"Yes?"

"They have prime rib here. Is it good?"

"I think it is."

"Wait there is no pricing on this menu!"

"That's the ladies menu; there are no prices on that menu."

"Then how am I supposed to know what to order?"

"Order what you like."

"But..."

"No buts; just tell me what you want and I'll order for us. Do you like prime rib?"

"I love prime rib, Benjamin. I'd do almost anything for prime rib."

"Prime rib it is," he said with a grin adding, "You might want to be careful about saying you'd do almost anything for prime rib."

"You know what I mean, Benjamin." She chided.

"As a matter of fact I don't know." He joked as he waved over the waiter who was waiting for his signal.

"It's just a figure of speech."

"Okay, I'll leave it at that." He smiled.

35

During dinner Ben began to briefly outline his travel itinerary, again, as a reminder to her. "They are all places I've been meaning to see. What do you think of the trip?"

"I think it would be a dream trip, absolutely!" she exclaimed.

Benjamin leaned across his prime rib to cover her hand with his. "I'm glad Jane, you like the idea."

After dinner, Benjamin and Jane waltzed to the band's renditions of the latest melodies; *Moon River*, *A Time for Us* and *All the Way*.

"There's a place I'd like to take you to tonight where the moon and stars appear close enough to touch. Would you like to go, Jane?"

"I'd love to."

"Good then, let's go."

Benjamin drove down an out-of- the-way country road , stopping at a closed gate. Reaching across Jane, he opened the glove box and took out a key. Jane looked at him questioningly.

"I know the owner, so I have a key to the gate and access to the land including the Ridge, our destination." He took off his tie, folded it and put the tie in the pocket of his suit jacket. Then he stepped outside of his car and took off his suit jacket and tossed the jacket in the back seat. "We're a little over-dressed for the Ridge, Jane,." he said in answer to her questioning looks.

After unlocking the gate and swinging it wide open, Bradley drove through then stopped, got out of his car, and locked the gate again. Back in the car, he drove through the field and around to the path that led to the back of the Ridge, a towering hill. The roughed-in road up the hill slipped in and around among the densely tree-covered landscape. Cautiously, Ben drove up the hill, stopping when he reached the far end of the flat top. Here Benjamin carefully turned his car around so that it was headed back towards the path they had just come up and then stopped and turned off the car.

Ben stepped out of the car and went around to the passenger's side and opened the door for Jane. "I think you'll see the night sky better out here," he said as he took her hand.

They walked away from the car. Looking up at the night sky, the sight was breathtaking. A field of twinkling stars stretched far across the dark blue velvet sky. They were as bright and sparkling as on a cold, clear winter's night. That night sky was further enhanced by the silvery moon that appeared close enough to touch.

"Is it as I said?"

"Oh, yes, Ben and more, it's so beautiful and so peaceful up here."

"Sometimes when I'm up here, I imagine hearing the wings of angels fluttering nearby."

"What a nice thought, Benjamin."

"More likely it's owls flying past." He smiled.

Benjamin placed his hands on Jane's shoulders and turned her so she faced him directly. "Jane, you look so beautiful." Under that bright starry night sky he kissed her long and passionately.

Later Benjamin slipped his arm around her waist and led her back to his car.

He opened the driver's side door for her. She slid over on the bench seat far enough so he would have room to sit. Once settled in the car Benjamin began unbuttoning his shirt as Jane leaned close to the windshield tilting her head skyward seemingly mesmerized by the celestial sight and unaware of Ben removing his shirt.

Again Ben's hands were on her shoulders turning her towards him drawing her close to his bare chest as he planted a long kiss on her lips. "Jane I've been wondering all evening why you pinned that shawl on over the top of your dress."

"Well this was the only dress I could find on sale in my size to wear to the Van Durham. But the bodice shows more cleavage than is decent.

"Oh, that reminds me! I have $33.72 in change for you after all my expenditures. Everything I bought was on sale." Jane turned to get the evening bag beside her to give Ben the change.

"Never mind, Jane. You can keep it."

"No"... She started to protest but his tone of voice left no room for debate. She kept the change.

"Do you mind if I judge whether you show too much cleavage?" Before Jane could answer Benjamin freed up his right hand and unclasped the large rhinestone pin holding the shawl together on her shoulder. He slipped the shawl off her and looked. "That's quite an invitation!"

Tossing the shawl into the back seat Benjamin took Jane in his arms and held her close as his lips covered her lips and with one hand he unzipped the back of her dress and unhooked her strapless bra. He pulled back enough to see what he had revealed. "They are beautiful, Jane!"

Before Jane could respond he pressed Jane's bare bosom into his naked, hairy chest and held her long. Still holding her against him, Benjamin whispered in her ear, "Jane, I love you, I truly love you."

Jane responded to him by saying, "Ben, you have a very nice manly chest."

Chapter 6 - In The Morning

Jane was alone in bed when the telephone rang. The bathroom door suddenly swung wide open as Bradley came barreling out of the bathroom with a large towel wrapped about his waist. "Dr. Bradley," he answered the telephone next to his bed.

"Just tell her I'll see her first when I make my rounds and if everything is all right I'll discharge her this morning." He chuckled as he replied to what the head nurse said next. "Tell you what Carol, if I think she cannot go home without professional help for a few days, I'll volunteer you as her private nurse,." he said as he sat down on the edge of his bed.

Even holding the telephone handset away from his ear Benjamin could clearly hear Carol loudly exclaim she would give up nursing before she'd be a private nurse for that ***** even for a day!

"Are you saying no to an opportunity?" He grinned.

"Yes!," the voice on the line boomed back.

"I'll be there in about an hour, Carol,." he said before hanging up the telephone.

Jane sat up, pulling the covers up around her. "Someone's not happy."

"That was the head nurse on the surgical floor. We have a patient that's never satisfied, always complaining. The kind the nurses would like to kill."

"There are always those patients, probably always will be." Changing the subject Jane noted, "You're up early." She yawned.

"Not early. It's almost 8 and I'm going to be late making my rounds."

"I thought you were off this weekend."

"I'm covering for Richardson until one or so this afternoon as a favor. So I'll be finishing up his rounds in Overlook Memorial Hospital, hopefully early this afternoon."

"Oh!" She exclaimed as Bradley kissed her. "You smell nice."

"Just showered and shaved."

"A shower sounds good."

"Why don't you take your shower while I make some coffee. Want some breakfast?"

"No breakfast, Ben, coffee yes, thanks."

"Suit yourself."

"Oh, that reminds me, where is my suitcase?"

"I'll bring it in here for you."

"Thank you."

"Ah wait," she said as he started to get up.

"What?"

"Just this", she said as she whipped off his towel. "I need something to get from here to the bathroom."

"You could've asked!" he exclaimed while pretending to be embarrassed as he sat back down on the edge of the bed.

"Would you have given me the towel if I asked?"

Grinning he answered, "No."

"Thanks again," Jane said as she wrapped the towel around her and slipped out of bed.

"Guess I'll get dressed," he called out to her back as she headed to the bathroom.

Showered and dressed, Jane joined Benjamin at the kitchen table. As Ben poured her coffee he pushed his plate of toast towards her. "Have some toast?"

"Really I'm not hungry, thanks. I ate so much last night I probably won't be hungry until tonight."

"You sure?"

"Absolutely."

Benjamin asked, "Do you have everything you need? Do you need to go shopping?"

"For what, I don't need anything."

"Some clothes, swim suit, that sort of thing or maybe night clothes?"

"Night clothes?"

"You know, those see through night clothes brides wear on their honeymoon."

"Do you mean negligees?" she smiled.

"Are they those flimsy things brides wear to titillate their already excited grooms?"

"I believe so." She laughed.

Smiling, he said, "Seems to me the easiest and cheapest thing to do is for the bride and groom to just take off all their clothes, hop into bed and get acquainted. That's better than wasting money on negligees."

"Not a whole lot of romance in that, I should think," Jane stated.

"The romance comes when they are under the covers."

"Oh does it?" she questioned.

"Of course," he declared with a grin.

"There are a couple of things I'd appreciate your picking up for me. I listed them on that paper." He pointed towards the center of the table where there was a sheet of paper and beside the paper there was money in an undetermined amount. "Why don't you go shopping for our trip and buy one of those negligees and anything else you want."

"What trip?" a surprised Jane asked.

"I told you I was going on vacation, have you forgotten?"

"No I haven't forgotten; but I thought I was going back to Chicago last night but then I thought it was too late to make it to the airport so I thought I would be going back today. I didn't think I was going on your trip with you."

"Jane, I want you to go on vacation with me. I've been alone for years and I don't want to be alone any more. I thought you understood that."

"I'm sorry, somehow that didn't register."

He reached across the table for her hand and clasped it as though he wouldn't let her go. "Jane, I told you I love you."

41

Jane carefully considered her next words. "Benjamin, I thought you said that out of the heat of passion and therefore you didn't mean it, so I didn't think it would be fair to hold you to that, so to speak."

"Jane, I meant it. I do love you and I want to marry you."

She looked genuinely surprised.

"Ben, you know I am very fond of you. I really missed you after you left Chicago and last night was very special for me, but we shouldn't feel obligated."

"Obligated, not obligated, Jane. I want you in my life as long as we live. That's not obligation, that's love,." he argued.

Jane fell silent as she gently slipped her hand out of his grasp and placed her elbows on the table creating a pyramid with her forearms as she locked her fingers together and balanced her chin on her outstretched thumbs and thought. Shortly, she collapsed her pyramid and looked directly into Benjamin Bradley's eyes.

"Ben," she spoke softly, "I am very fond of you. I believe I love you. But I need to be perfectly honest. You remember I told you I had brought Matt to the airport a week before you arrived?"

"Yes," Ben replied as he braced himself for what he was sure would be unwanted news.

"I, I…" Jane began hesitantly. "Well, my periods are not regular, never have been. "This past month especially, my life has been full of complications and emotional strain so a delay isn't all that surprising but..."

"Jane," Benjamin broke in, "Are you trying to tell me you might be pregnant?"

"It's a possibility." She answered as her eyes dropped away from his face.

Ben quietly stood up and moved away from the table and leaned against the kitchen sink. "And if you are, what will you do?" he asked looking straight at her.

"I have options," she stated, hoping that would be the end of the subject.

"Such as?" he pushed.

"You know I am a qualified doctor. I can go back to Chicago and work as a General Practitioner; I have my license to practice medicine in Illinois, and I'm Board Certified," she added to strengthen her defense.

"Or, I can go back home take my exams and work in Indiana. And, of course I could go to Germany."

It was Bradley's turn to look surprised. "You mean you would join what's his name in Germany? Why and how would you find him?"

"Finding him wouldn't be hard. Matt called my parents the day after you left Chicago, asking when I would be home. He wanted to be there when I arrived.

"My father told him he didn't know when I would be home, so Matt gave Dad his telephone number in Germany so I could contact him."

"I thought you were through with him!"

"A father has the right to know and should know he has a child. So, if I am, then he needs to know and I'm sure he would want me to be with him."

Even as she spoke Jane wasn't sure she would follow through on her spoken convictions.

"Did the hospital pay for my plane ticket and hotel room?" Jane asked.

Thoroughly surprised by the changed subject, he answered without thinking,. "No."

"You did?"

"Yes."

Suddenly, there was absolute silence between them. Then again, without thinking, Bradley asked, "How many times?"

"What?" Jane was stunned by his question.

"How many times?" He repeated, again not thinking while surprising even himself at his question.

Shocked, Jane snapped back as she understood the question. "How dare you! That's a question I wouldn't ask anyone. I see no reason to do so."

Quickly coming to her feet, she made no attempt to conceal her anger. "Don't you need to rescue the nurses on the surgical floor, and see if you can discharge that pain in the neck patient? Do your rounds? You're late, aren't you?"

"Guess I better go," he replied meekly.

"That's a good idea," she retorted.

Before he turned to leave, he said, "I would appreciate your picking up those things for me. There should be enough money for cab fare too; if not, page me at the hospital and I'll come pick you up."

"Have a good time," she said as he reached the door. He turned with a puzzled look on his face, not understanding the meaning behind her parting remark. But, he said nothing and went out the door. Jane had decided she would not be going anywhere with Benjamin Bradley, not then, not ever.

Hearing the Genie Door Opener lift the garage door up, Jane stepped over to the kitchen sink and looked out the window and watched as his car pulled out of the garage and moved down the driveway and on to the road.

Sure he was on his way, Jane quickly searched for and found the telephone book. She made three calls. An airline ticket cost more money than she had, so flying back to Chicago was out. Her next call was to the bus terminal. The news there was encouraging;, she could afford a ticket.

On the last call she asked, "How much will that be?" Then she asked, "Can I be picked up..." she glanced up at the clock, "by 11:30 this morning?"

The dispatcher's reply was a firm yes.

"Thank you. I'll be ready," she added before hanging up the telephone.

Quickly, Jane went into action. First in the master bedroom she made up the bed and in the bathroom she picked up. In the kitchen she rinsed the breakfast dishes and put them in the dishwasher and made sure the kitchen was clean. While she was picking up, the telephone rang. At first she thought of picking it up, but then the thought of trying to talk to Bradley at the moment was more than she was willing to handle and she decided to ignore the rings.

Back in the bedroom, Jane flung open her suitcase and took out the boxes she had carefully folded and had planned on tossing in the trash later. She neatly put the clothing and the accessories she had bought the day before in the appropriate boxes along with the receipts, all except the under garments.

Seeing all was in order, she returned to the kitchen. On the table was the sheet of paper folded in half next to the money Benjamin had left for her. On the paper she wrote:

"Dear Dr. Bradley,

Thank you for a very nice week. I have decided to return to Chicago. I will send a thank-you note to your Board for the interview and explain that I've changed my mind and will accept the residency in Chicago.

You will find the dress, shoes, evening bag, and the rhinestone jewelry together on your bed with the receipts so you can either take them back to the store or save them for your next female guest. I threw out the under garments. You can probably get your money back on the return plane ticket to Chicago, I left it here along with all the money you had on this table.

I will pay you back for all the expenses I've incurred coming here, as soon as I can. I promise. Dr. Jane Potts"

Chapter 7 - Cold Uncertainty

It was a cold rain that poured down late that afternoon when a very tall, white- haired man stepped into the main waiting room of the Greyhound Bus terminal in Overlook.

Jane was easy to spot with only a handful of people scattered about the terminal waiting area. She was the only one in the front row of seats, apparently absorbed in a paperback.

He walked over to her and sat down next to her. She never looked up to see who was beside her, so when Bradley spoke her name he startled her.

Seeing him beside her stirred up her anger. "What are you doing here?"

"I need to talk to you."

"I don't think there is anything to talk about. So you can leave, now."

"Jane, please I really need to talk to you."

She heaved a heavy sigh as she glanced at her watch. "It's a little after four; my bus leaves at six and I intend to be on that bus. So whatever you have to say, say it now."

"Jane, I would like to talk to you privately, not here in public."

Deciding Bradley would not leave until he had his say Jane reluctantly asked, "Where do you want to talk?"

"In my car."

Jane looked down at her book, her thumb holding the place. Carefully she folded the corner of the page and closed the book.

"All right." She said as she got up and started to grab the handle of her suitcase.

Benjamin was quicker. He took the handle of her suitcase saying, "I'll carry it."

In the car, Benjamin turned the key in the ignition.

"Where do you think you're going?" She bristled.

"Nowhere. It's cold and I have to start up the car in order to turn on the heat."

"Oh."

"You don't trust me, do you?"

"No, I don't," she stated flatly.

"That's not a good beginning, is it?"

"No, it isn't, so why don't we say good-bye now and be done with it," she suggested coldly.

"Because I believe if you leave now we'll both live to regret it and I don't want to live the rest of my life regretting your loss."

"I'm sorry, Dr. Bradley, but that's the way it's going to have to be. I have no doubt you can find someone else. And soon, since your libido has been reawakened. So my best to you, and your future, whomever!" She spouted as she reached for the door handle.

"No, wait." Again Bradley's hand was quicker than hers as he reached over her and firmly took her hand off the door handle. "You aren't being fair, Jane and your sarcasm is grating. So try to listen, and forget the sarcasm."

Since Jane said nothing, Bradley began, "I don't know why I asked that question, it wasn't even in my mind. It just came out. I can't explain it. It was not relevant. I tried calling you from the hospital but when you didn't answer I thought you were thinking it could be someone other than me, and you didn't want to try to explain being in my house. I could understand that. But then when I came home and called to you and you didn't answer, I felt all alone, again.

"Then I read your note and it cut deep into my heart. All of this because of a few words, and no chance to say I'm sorry and you are leaving? You told me you loved me. I believed you. I didn't chalk it up to the heat of passion."

"Did you discharge that annoying patient?"

"Yes, why are you changing the subject, Jane?"

"What is it you want from me, Dr. Bradley?"

47

"Don't call me Dr. Bradley, that's cold. What I want from you is to come back home with me so we can talk about getting married. I love you Jane; if I didn't love you, I wouldn't have gone looking for you."

"I don't think it's a good idea that I go with you. You don't need me to complicate your life, and I don't want to be a burden to you, and I don't want regrets for either one of us."

"You wouldn't be a burden Jane, because I love you. Besides, I've always wanted children, Jane, but I couldn't have them with Luanne so I would gladly give the baby my name and raise him as my own. If that's what you're worried about."

There was something about his telling her he couldn't have children with his first wife that struck Jane. Later she would remember what he said under different circumstances.

Jane fell silent feeling she was losing her defense. Now she wasn't sure how she felt about Benjamin, or what she should do, so she ventured, "I have enough money for my ticket. So I'll go and you'll forget about me and I you."

"I won't forget you, Jane, and I wouldn't want you to forget me. I promise if you will go back home with me now and by tomorrow, if you still insist upon going back to Chicago, I'll drive you to this bus terminal or take you to the airport and pay for your flight back to Chicago, which ever you want. You can trust me, Jane."

"Somehow I don't think you'll let me out of this car unless I go back with you. So I'll go back with you but I don't think it will do much good."

"We'll see," he said.

Jane sighed as she leaned back in the seat thinking she had lost control of her life. Closing her eyes, she wondered where she would be a year from now, but more importantly she wondered how she really felt about Benjamin Franklin Bradley.

Ben drove in silence. The persistent rain, the sounds of the windshield wipers scraping across the windshield and the warm air blowing from the car's heater made Jane drowsy, her eye lids grew heavy. A little while later she felt the car begin to slow down. It seemed too soon to be in Glenwood. She opened her eyes and looked around then turned to Benjamin. "Why are you slowing down?"

"There's a diner here that has carry out. I'm hungry, so I thought I'd get us something and we can eat at home. What do you want?"

"I'm not very hungry."

Ben heaved a quiet sigh. "Jane, don't be difficult. Just tell me what you would like."

"Anything, I'm not fussy, something light, not much."

"All right I'll get us something, unless you want to eat inside."

Jane glared at him. "I don't think so."

"Okay, I'll be back," he said as he stepped out into the rain.

It was quiet on the trip back to Benjamin's house. The supper was warm, filling with little talk between the two. After supper Benjamin lit a fire in the fireplace.

Once the two were seated in the parlor on the sofa in front of the fire, Benjamin began. "What is it about me you don't like, Jane?"

Jane shrugged her shoulders and said nothing.

Benjamin persisted. "Do you think I'm too old for you?"

She looked at him and said, "No, of course not."

"Then what is it, Jane? You can't still hold that stupid question against me. I told you I didn't know why I asked. I really don't. Can't you forgive me a few stupid words? Haven't you ever said something or questioned something that you realized afterwards was stupid and did not reflect you or your thoughts?"

"I'm sure I have. I just don't like to look back at my mistakes."

49

"You're forcing me to do just that and worse, dwell on what I said. Jane, I told you I was sorry and I meant it. Just as I meant it when I told you I love you and want to marry you. Don't be obstinate Jane, don't give us both something to regret for the rest of our lives."

Suddenly Jane was struck with the memories and feelings she had when she left Midway Airport and how lonely and sad she felt because Ben had left Chicago. Jane turned and faced Ben. "I guess I am being too hard on you. I'm sorry, Ben."

Benjamin's face lit up., He kissed her and asked,. "Will you marry me? I love you, Jane. I really love you."

Time stopped and began again when Jane finally answered Benjamin. "Yes, I will marry you, Ben; because the truth is, I love you too."

With a smile, Benjamin reached in his pocket and brought out a blue velvet-covered ring box and opened it. The sight of the ring caused Jane to catch her breath.

"I bought it in Chicago that last Saturday I was there."

Jane remembered how she thought Ben had a secret that Saturday night in Chicago. Now, she knew his secret was he had bought her an engagement ring. "I've been waiting for the right time to give it to you," he was saying.

"It's beautiful, Ben!"

Benjamin was pleased to see she was happy with his choice of a ring for her. "I bought the wedding band to match. I'll give that to you when you say 'I do.' I also bought a wedding band for you to place on my finger when I say 'I do.'"

"Aren't I supposed to buy your ring?"

"Knowing the small amount of money interns make, I didn't think you would have an extra twenty-five dollars or so to spend on a ring. And, I didn't want to wait for you to buy me a ring. I only hoped you wouldn't mind if I purchased it."

"I don't mind, but somehow I'll make it up to you. Do you have a date you want to marry?"

"As a matter of fact, I was thinking when we are in Nevada. That's where we can start our honeymoon. Is that all right with you?"

Without hesitation she answered, "Yes."

"There is one more thing we have to consider."

"What's that?"

Benjamin began, "If you are pregnant, Jane, we will have to tell and live with a lie to protect our reputations and that of the child. We will have to say we eloped while I was in Chicago and never tell anyone we didn't get married until we landed in Nevada. Do you agree?"

It was then that Jane was beginning to realize how much Benjamin Franklin Bradley loved her; he was ready and willing to protect her with his impeccable reputation and lie for her. Jane was both astounded and appreciative. "Yes, I agree, thank you Ben, you are very thoughtful."

"We need to be at the airport tomorrow morning at 8:45."

"Okay," she answered.

On Monday morning June 2, 1958 his Honor Jacques Lemont, a municipal Judge in Reno, Nevada married Benjamin and Jane. Benjamin rented a station wagon for their travels. Before leaving Nevada they spent several hours touring south of Reno and ended up spending some time in Las Vegas playing the slot machines. It was Jane, who while playing the fifty dollars Benjamin gave her to gamble with, hit the jackpot for three thousand dollars. It was more money than she had ever seen.

Benjamin and Jane traveled leisurely and in comfort along their route from the Desert in Nevada to the Rocky Mountains and beyond, that included a stop in Indiana.

The only unexpected turn in their plans came the day after they were married. Jane announced she needed to find a drugstore.

In their room, Benjamin asked, "How long will it last?"

51

"Four or five days," she answered and asked, "Aren't you happy about this? I am."

"I wish it had held off a few more days. We just got married," he complained.

"Ben, there will be plenty of time later."

Chapter 8 - Family

It was before dawn, two weeks later when Ben asked Jane, "Are you sure we're on the right road?"

"Yes, it's a long way and that's why I suggested you fill up the gas tank at that last filling station. You don't want to run out of gas out here."

What seemed like hours later Jane pointed to the right, "Turn here, Ben."

"That looks like a dirt road."

"It is and it runs along the front of my parents' farm."

"How far from here?"

"About ten miles."

Ben could hear the excitement in Jane's voice as they neared her family's farm. "I hope your parents won't be too upset with me for not calling about our getting married."

"Frankly Ben, I think they will be so happy to see us, they won't be upset at all."

"I still think you should give them the money you won. Call it a dowry or money instead of gifts, Jane."

Daylight was about to break when they pulled into the front yard of the Potts farmhouse. Ben and Jane crossed the porch and into the kitchen without disturbing the sleeping couple.

Scooter woke up as they entered the dark kitchen but before he could bark a warning Jane placed a quieting hand on the back of his neck assuring him she belonged there. His bushy white tail wagged crazily as he realized who was home.

Speaking quietly, Jane told Ben, "I'll take him with me so he won't bother you. He'll be fine once he knows you." Jane switched on the over head kitchen light. "You better stay here. I'll make sure my Dad doesn't bring out his shot gun." Grinning she turned on the hallway light before moving down the hallway towards her parent's bedroom with her hand on the big dog's neck.

She knocked on her parents' bedroom door as she called to them. "Dad, Mom."

Her father was the first to respond. "Who's there?"

"It's me Dad, Jane."

Excitedly her father called out, "I'll be right there! Margie, Margie wake up! Our Jane's home! Come on hurry up!" he urged his wife.

In the next moment the door swung wide open and her father's arms were around her. He planted a kiss on her check as he exclaimed., "Jane, you're home! Why didn't you let us know you were coming?"

"We wanted to surprise you and mom."

Looking puzzled, her father asked, "Who are we?" But before she could answer her mother was in the hallway too.

"Jane," Scott Potts stepped aside as Marjorie embraced their daughter. "Let's go into the kitchen." Marjorie suggested.

Scooter bounded down the hallway ahead of the three of them. As they entered the kitchen Ben was caught peeking under the clean cloth that was covering two loaves of bread and Scooter was sitting on the floor beside his new friend, Ben.

"Ben." Hearing his wife address him Ben turned around and met his in-laws more than halfway in the large country kitchen with his hand out.

"Dad, Mon this is Benjamin Franklin Bradley, my husband." Jane introduced her husband in a slow, soft voice to her surprised parents.

After a brief and embarrassing delay, Jane's father accepted Ben's hand and they shook hands. Marjorie smiled as she nodded a friendly welcome to Ben and asked, "Are you hungry, Benjamin?"

"It's been a long drive and if you don't mind coffee would be fine Ah", Ben jerked his thumb in the direction of the covered bread and asked, "Did you make that bread?"

"Yes," Marjorie answered with a warm smile. "We'll have some with breakfast, Benjamin, toasted, if you like."

54

Glancing up at the kitchen clock, Marjorie said "We would have gotten up in about an hour, so I'll make breakfast now. Sit down, Ben make yourself at home. You too, Jane."

"Do you want some help, Mom?' Jane asked.

"No thanks, you sit down too, Jane. Have you been driving all day?" She asked as she moved about preparing to make breakfast.

"Ben's been doing all the driving I've just tried to stay awake. We wanted to be here today, it has been a very long drive," Jane answered.

"Seems to me, you two have a lot to tell us," Scott Potts stated as he sat down across the table from the newlyweds.

"What do you want to know, Dad?"

"First, why didn't you tell us you were going to be married, Jane?"

"That's my fault, Mr. Potts," Benjamin answered. "I know I should have called you and asked you for Jane's hand. I apologize for not calling you. But there were two problems, one you didn't know me and the other was it was tough getting her to agree to marry me. I promised her if she married me we would come visit you both during our honeymoon. I'm keeping my promise now."

Scott Potts had his elbow on the table with his hand under his chin and looked impressed with Benjamin's explanation as he lifted his eyebrows and proffered a brief smile.

"What do you do for a living, Benjamin?" he asked.

"I'm a surgeon and the Hospital Administrator at Switzer Memorial Hospital in Glenwood, New York."

"He's also the chairman of the Intern and Resident's Program at Switzer's," Jane butted in.

The father looked at his daughter. "If you were in Chicago and Benjamin in New York, how did you come to meet?"

"I applied to Switzer for their Pediatrics Residency Program and Ben flew to Chicago to interview me before I went before the Board."

"Isn't that a little unusual?" he asked looking at Benjamin.

"Well, your daughter has a great academic record that was very impressive, her letters of reference were outstanding and her introductory letter was personable and appealing and her photograph also caught my attention.

"So, I called her and told her I would like to meet her in the hospital where she was doing her internship. Frankly, I fell in love with her right away. So, I decided I had to marry her."

Marjorie smiled at the love story as she handed the first breakfast plate to Benjamin. Just as she started to fill the next plate the telephone rang. "I bet that's Josh," she said.

Scott was up on his feet, with his hand on the receiver by the time the telephone rang twice. "Hello," he answered.

On the other end of the line a voice said, "Hello, Dad."

"Morning Josh, what are you doing up so early? You've got another hour of sleep coming to you."

"I was thinking of making my breakfast. I'm really hungry this morning, but I was looking across the way and saw your lights on, anything the matter?"

"No, we just had a nice surprise come walking in."

"Who?"

"Your sister."

"Jane? About time she came home!"

"She didn't come alone."

"Who is with her?"

"Her husband."

"Her husband! I'll be right over!" Scott chuckled as he heard the click on the other end of the line.

"Your brother is on his way over," he said to Jane and to his wife, "You better put on another plate, Josh said he was hungry. Besides I need some help today!"

56

Looking at Jane he added with a grin, "A little bribery goes a long way with your brother."

Scooter started barking as Josh landed on the porch. The door swung open and in walked a tall, lean, muscular-looking man. Josh Potts arrived just as the last breakfast plate was on the table, his plate. He immediately went over to where his sister sat and threw his arms around her, lifting her out of her chair, and kissed her. "'Bout time you came home, Sis. Thought we were going to have to go to Chicago and bring you home." In the next breath he questioned, "Dad said you are married?"

"Yes I am." Jane turned to Ben. "Ben this is my big brother, Josh. Josh, this is my husband Benjamin Franklin Bradley." Ben stood up as Jane began the introduction and extended his hand to Josh Potts. Josh shook Ben's hand.

"Did I hear right, is it Benjamin Franklin Bradley?"

"Yes," Ben answered.

"You aren't related to The Benjamin Franklin?"

Ben smiled, "I am."

Josh eyes widened. "Really, where are you from?"

"I was born and raised in Philadelphia. Benjamin Franklin is my grandfather to the tenth generation on my mother's side."

"Wow, you know I teach American History? Having a brother-in-law related to Benjamin Franklin should give me some prestige in the eyes of my students!" He smiled broadly.

Grinning, Ben said, "Jane told me you taught history and that you might have some questions about Grandfather Ben, for me."

"Just give me some time and I'll come up with a list, if you don't mind."

"I'll try to answer your questions. If I can't, I know the curators of some of the museums that have impressive displays on him and they probably can help."

"Fair enough, thank you."

"Sit down, Josh, and eat while it's still hot."

57

"Thanks Mom. So what do you do for a living, Ben?"

"I'm a surgeon."

"Oh, that makes sense. Is that how you met my sister? Do you practice in Philadelphia?"

"No, Glenwood, New York."

"New York! My sister has been in Chicago, how...?"

His father interrupted, "Don't bother with questions now Josh, we already have the answers. Listen, how busy are you today, Josh?"

"What do you need done, Dad?"

"Well I have a list..."

"Sure you do," Josh chuckled.

"Mom, what's for supper tonight?" Josh asked.

"I don't know yet."

"Jane, something you'd like, Honey?" Marjorie asked her daughter.

"Mom, I'd love a roast turkey."

"Josh, you've got a fat old lady over there. Why don't we take her? Scott Potts suggested.

"Dad, you shouldn't be talking about my mother-in-law like that! She wouldn't like that and she could make you very unhappy, if she heard you!" Josh Potts chuckled.

Jane burst into laughter and would have spilled her coffee had not Ben caught her cup.

"I meant that fat old turkey that's always nipping at you."

"That's the one, she's got a name too!" Josh was laughing so hard he didn't hear the telephone.

"Josh, telephone!" His mother called.

"Hello, no, everything is all right. It's my sister she's home. She just got here. No, I didn't know she was coming. I don't think so, Honey, she and her husband are eating breakfast. Yes, I did say... We're all eating over here tonight. Mom's going to roast turkey. I've got to bring over the old turkey, before I start my chores. I'll be here most of the day. My Dad has a list of things I have to help him with. I don't know, Lisa, ask her. Okay, just a minute."

"Mom, Lisa wants to talk to you." Josh handed the phone to his Mother then took his place at the table.

"So, do you have any outlaws, I mean in-laws, Jane?" Josh grinned as he asked that question.

"No, Josh, unfortunately Ben's parents died in a train wreck years ago and he is an only child."

"Oh, I am sorry, Ben." Josh said seriously.

"Thank you, Josh."

Marjorie Potts cradled the telephone hand piece and sat down at the table. "Lisa wanted to know what she could make for dinner tonight. She'll be over later on."

Just as she finished speaking, Marjorie happened to see a sparkle. "Oh, my Jane." she exclaimed as she clasped her daughter's hand. "What beautiful rings! You don't need a magnifying glass to see those diamonds. Did you pick out those rings, Benjamin?"

"Yes, I did. I bought them in Chicago and gave her the engagement ring in New York and the wedding band in Nevada where we were married. I could only hope she would like them."

"She would be a darn fool is she didn't," Scott Potts piped up and Josh agreed.

"I think they are beautiful," Jane stated. "Glad everyone likes them."

"I hate to mention it, but I'm tired. We've been on the road for almost twenty-four hours. We could use some sleep. Mom, is my room available?" Jane asked.

"Of course."

"Sheets?"

"In your room."

"Thanks Mom." Jane turned to Ben. "Why don't we get our luggage?"

"I'll help you, Ben," Josh offered.

Jane headed upstairs as Ben and Josh headed outside.

Seeing all the boxes in the back of the station wagon, Josh questioned, "You brought all these boxes with you from New York?"

"No, we stopped in Chicago before coming here. We had to clear out Jane's things from her room in the dorm. Most of the boxes contain her books, notes, letters she still has to answer, and a couple of lamps."

Laughing, Ben recalled, "It was over her car that we almost caused a scene in the dorm's parking lot. I made her give her car to a starving resident. He was someone she didn't like. When I promised to buy her a station wagon when we get back to Glenwood, she gave up her clunker, peacefully!"

"That sounds like my sister! She can be very obstinate even when she's wrong!" Chuckling, Josh added, "Well at least you got her to give in. I have to admire you for that! Usually Dad is the only one who can get her to back off her obstinate attitude!"

Upstairs Jane had just finished making up her bed with fresh-smelling air-dried sheets when Ben brought in their luggage.

Yawning, Jane said to Ben, "I'm ready to jump into bed. Oh, and the bathroom is across the hall."

"I'll be right back."

In the mean time Jane had changed and was in bed by the time Ben came back.

"Do I need to put on pajamas?"

"That would be a good idea. My nephews might come barreling in when they get here."

Stretching, he said, "Okay..."

Jane turned on her side and watched while Ben undressed. "You know, Ben, if I wasn't so tired I'd take a shot at seducing you. You are so tempting naked."

"Can't say much for your timing, Jane, but I love you anyway and I'll take a rain check on that seducing business, although you'll find me easy to seduce," he grinned as he got into bed.

"Ben, you really are the best that could have happen to me."

"Does that mean you love me, Jane?"

60

"Yes, I do love you Ben, big time."

It was a sleep of peaceful dreams and pleasant hopes that were suddenly interrupted by loud whispers. It took a couple of seconds for Ben to open and then focus his eyes on two little boys that looked exactly alike. He smiled when he heard one of them say, "That's Uncle Ben, he is a big fellow." The other little boy shook his head in agreement.

"Hello," Ben said.

"Hello, Uncle Ben, we are Josh Potts' little boys."

Ben swung out of the bed. Sitting on the edge of the bed, he extended his hand to the little boys. The first twin said, "I'm Jeremiah Josh Potts," as Ben shook his hand. Following his brother's example the other little boy extended his hand to Uncle Ben and said, "I'm John Josh Potts." After shaking hands a voice behind Benjamin asked, "Anyone going to say hello to Aunt Jane?"

Jane moved around from behind Ben. Seeing her, the boys climbed up into the bed and into Jane's waiting arms.

Chapter 9 - The Mystery Woman

"Isn't that Doc Bradley's Oldsmobile?" The teenager asked as he looked out of the Overlook meat market's storefront window. Behind the register his mother looked at where he was pointing.

"I think so."

"Whoa, that's not Doc Bradley getting out of the car. Hey Dad, come here look at this," he called to his father who was removing the orange paper from the meat in the refrigerated cases.

Suddenly the mother turned to her son and said, "Go help your father. She's coming this way."

Dennis Band met his father on his way to the back of the store. "She's coming in here, Dad." Father and son quickly moved in behind the meat counter and watched as the door opened.

"Good morning!" Jane cheerfully called out to the lady who appeared to be intent on filling the gum rack next to the register.

"Good morning," Shirley Band replied as she turned and faced the new customer.

"Am I too early, are you open?"

"You aren't too early, we're open, just getting ready for the day. It will probably be busy today with everyone getting ready for the Fourth." She smiled as Jane nodded in agreement.

"Then I had better get moving." Jane glanced about as she walked over to the meat counter. "Good morning," she greeted father and son with a smile.

"Good morning," the father responded, smiling. "What can I get you?"

She looked down at the list in her hand and began rattling off her meat order. "Two boneless chicken breasts, one pound of ground beef, four hot dogs, a quarter of a pound…"

"Whoa, that's a little fast for me."

"Oh I'm sorry."

"That's ok. Would you like me to take your list and fill the order?"

"That would be great, thank you. I need to order some cold cuts too and two steaks. I'll have to ask what kind of steaks so we'll order those last."

Just then Benjamin blew into the meat market like a whirlwind and stopped next to Jane. "Jane, do you have my wallet?"

"No."

"Good morning, Doc."

Benjamin glanced over to the meat counter. "Oh, good morning, Tucker."

"Something wrong, Doc?" the butcher asked.

"No, just can't find my wallet."

Benjamin turned back to Jane. "Did you take it?"

"No, I have this..." She pulled out a money clip from a pocket in her Bermuda shorts. "You told me to take your money clip."

"Do you have your wallet with you?"

"No, I left my hand bag home, I didn't think I would need it."

"Ben, you probably left your wallet in the trousers you wore yesterday."

"Hope that's where it is," Bradley said.

Suddenly he smiled as he asked, "So, shall we flip a coin to see who is going home to get my wallet?"

"No, I'm not playing that game. I didn't misplace your wallet."

"All right...I'm going to the bank. It's just a couple of buildings down from here."

Smiling broadly, Jane asked, "What are you going to do, rob it?"

"No, I'm going to get some money out of my account. They know me over there."

"All you have to do is go over to the bank ask for money and you can get it!" she exclaimed then asked. "Can I do that?"

"No, you cannot!" he firmly pointed out.

Just as he was about to turn around, Jane asked,. "Ben, did you go to the grocer's yet?"

"Yes, that's why I need some money. He had rung up our groceries and put them in bags before I realized I didn't have my wallet."

"Here take this money." She held out the money clip, "and pay for the groceries before you go to the bank. This way you won't hold up the grocer. But you have to come here after you go to the bank so we can pay for the meat," she reminded him.

Taking the money clip out of her hand he was about to turn and leave when she said "Oh, Ben, will you get enough money so I can go to the bakery?"

"Yup," he answered and left the market without another word.

Jane was smiling to herself as she thought about the scene with Ben. She had no doubt that she and Benjamin had been a form of entertainment for the two men behind the meat counter, and the woman behind the register, who she was sure, had been listening too.

Seeing the two men behind the meat counter busy putting up her order, she slowly walked up to the register. At the register there were two colorful pinwheels on display. Jane picked one up and blew gently on it and like a child she watched, with delight, it spin and dazzle the eyes with its whirling colors.

"Excuse me; are these pinwheels for sale?"

"Yes, they are five cents each."

"I'll take this one. And the sparklers, how much are those?"

"They are ten cents a box."

"Oh good, I'll take a box. Thank you. Oh, and I think I'll take a package of Juicy Fruit gum, one Teaberry, one

Cloves, one Beemans and one Blackjack gum. Now all I have to do is wait for Ben."

Shirley Band noticed the sparkle on the mystery woman's left hand and was trying to think of a tactful way to ask the burning question when her husband came up behind Jane with her order in a box and placed it on the counter.

"Oh, thank you. I forgot to give you the order for the cold cuts."

"You had what you wanted written on the back of your note."

"Oh, that's right, thank you, I'm glad you noticed. Now I need to ask Ben what he wants for steaks."

"I gave him two T-bones I know he'll like. But, if he doesn't, I'll take care of it."

"Thank you so much, I appreciate it." Just as Jane was about to make another appreciative comment on the service, a man stepped into the meat market. He glanced over at the threesome standing at the register and smiled as he walked over to the counter where they were and looked at Jane in particular. He raised his eyebrows in recognition. "Dr. Jane Potts."

Jane answered immediately, "Yes," as she looked into the stranger's face and recognized Dr. Ken Richardson, a surgeon representing Overlook Memorial Hospital on the Admittance Board and who had asked her some tough questions during her interview. She smiled.

"So what are you doing here?"

"Buying meat for the Fourth, and you?"

"Doing the same. Can I give you my list, Tucker?" he asked as he turned to Tucker who was obviously listening to their conversation.

"Sure, everybody else does." He grinned.

"Great, thanks," Richardson said as he handed the butcher his list. "So, when are you coming on board, Jane?"

65

"On the fourteenth along with the rest of the residents". Just then she looked out the window. "Oh good, here comes Ben."

"What's Ben doing?"

"Hopefully he's coming to pay this bill."

"How come?"

"Because he forgot his wallet at home and he had to go to the bank to get some money."

Aware that Shirley Band was listening to their conversation, Richardson moved to block Shirley's view of Jane and him when he quietly asked, "You're staying with Ben?"

To his astonishment, Jane showed no embarrassment as she smiled and answered in the affirmative.

"Well, I have to go to the grocer while Tucker's getting the meat for me. So I'll see you at the hospital. Have a nice Fourth, Jane," he said as he waved and walked towards the door.

"Thank you, you too," she called after him.

From the store window Jane could see the two men exchanged brief greetings as they passed each other.

In a moment Ben was in the store he looked at his wife and asked, "Are we all set?"

"Yes, just need you to pay." Having finished their business in the meat market, Ben and Jane stood outside talking.

"I'll take the rental car and go straight home. Do you still want to go to the bakery?"

Jane answered, "Yes," and took the replenished money clip from Ben.

"So, you won't be long?"

"No, Ben I won't be. See you at home." She waved to him.

Jane walked fast in the bright sunlight past the two shop doors to the bakery. There were a few people sitting at the tables having coffee and doughnuts and a few others standing along the counter. It wasn't long before Jane was waited on, her shopping was done and she was on her way home.

Back in the meat market the family of three had gathered up front for a conference. "Who is she?" Tucker asked his wife.

"I don't know. I was going to ask her when you brought her order over."

"Maybe she's Doc Bradley's wife," the son suggested.

"No, that other Doctor called her by another name, Potts, I think. Apparently she's a doctor too." His mother stated. "She's married to somebody. You should have seen her rings. Her engagement ring didn't come out of any Five and Dime."

"So what's Bradley doing with her?" Tucker asked.

His wife giggled. "Maybe he's shacking up with her! She knew where his wallet was."

For a small town there was a lot of traffic coming into town and going out of town. Once Jane maneuvered the car into a line, it was hurry up and wait as the line going out of town appeared to be stalled. Finally the outward-bound traffic began to move. At the first traffic light several cars ahead of her took the right hand turn. Now she was closer to the front of the traffic lane heading outside of town. When she moved up to the second traffic light she noticed a couple of cars took the left hand turn. The car in front looked like Ben's rental car with Ben driving it. By the time Jane had reached the traffic signal the light turned yellow. She took a chance on the caution light and turned off to the left.

Ben and the car behind him had out distanced her in a hurry. She wondered what was wrong. For a moment she almost lost sight of Ben because he had turned again off the road to the left on to a road that dipped downward.

Jane slowed down to get her bearings. There were no cars behind her and the car that had been in front of her was sailing along the road up ahead, apparently with no intentions of turning off any time soon.

67

Slowly, Jane approached the turn-off Ben had taken. She took the turn cautiously, looking all around to see where Ben was. Off to the right was a cemetery. From the height of the land she spotted Ben's rental car. For a long moment Jane pressed down hard on the brakes as she stared at the car stopped in front of a mausoleum. As she stared she hoped that she had made a mistake and that was not Benjamin. She closed her eyes and gripped the steering wheel tighter. When she opened her eyes she saw the car she had followed was driving away.

Jane carefully lifted her foot off the brake and let the car slowly roll the rest of the way down the hill. She was sure she knew where the car had parked and followed her mental directions as she saw the rental car leave that place of the dead.

Finally, Jane pulled up in front of the place she was sure the car had parked. Reluctantly she turned and looked at the mausoleum. What she was dreading to see was there in bold letters at the top just below the rim of the roof, "Bradley." Midway down on the right hand panel was the name Luanne and the date she was born and the date she died.

In front of the mausoleum was a large stone urn. In the urn stood a tall metal vase containing two dozen fresh cut long stem yellow roses with baby's breath mixed with the roses giving the appearance of a bridal bouquet. Jane slowly exhaled the air she had unconsciously held. In the silence of her heart she hurt.

Jane did not know why but her eyes moved upward to the peak of the mausoleum. Within that small space between the peak and the top horizontal line was carved, "Love is forever."

Catching her breath she took off her engagement ring and then her wedding band. Inside the slightly wide band was scrolled, "Jane, Love is forever. Ben."

On the way to Benjamin's house Jane's thoughts ran in many directions. None of those thoughts were comforting.

Jane pulled into the driveway. While getting out of the car she remembered she had the bakery goods and the box of meat. The front door was open so she carried in the box of meat first. Ben was nowhere in sight so she went out to get the bakery goods. Not at all anxious to face Ben she made a slow return into the house.

"Jane," Ben called from the bedroom.

"Yes, Ben?"

"Will you come in here so we can pack?"

Chapter 10 - The Fishing Trip

Jane moved along into the bedroom. On the bed was what looked like a large duffle bag. Ben was pulling out some things from his dresser. "Jane, will you get out the clothes you want for the next three or four days."

"This bag is all the room we have for clothes so you can't pack too much. You better bring a sweater and a jacket. It can get cold on the lake."

"How about towels, blankets, sheets, do we need to bring those?" she asked.

"No, they are on the boat. All we have to pack is our clothes and bring some food."

"Soaps, shampoos, tooth brushes, tooth paste?" she asked as she fought back the pain-filled questioning thoughts that wanted answers.

"Ah yes, but just pack those things for yourself. I have my shaving kit and it has all I need in it."

"It's supposed to rain late this afternoon, so we need to get moving. I'll want to dock before we have a torrential down pour"

Jane had no knowledge of boating or terms associated with it and had no idea what he meant about docking, but she rushed about putting together the things she wanted to take. She placed them on the bed and stood back and watched Benjamin tightly fold their clothes and expertly stuff the duffle bag.

As Jane watched Ben, the three words at the top of the mausoleum flashed in her mind. Quietly she walked over to her dresser and took off her engagement ring and wedding band and put them in the back of the top middle drawer and left the bedroom.

At that moment Jane did not know where she stood with Ben. That he should have flowers for his dead wife and put them in front of her final resting place just a few hours before he and his second wife were about to leave on the last leg of their honeymoon was troubling to Jane. She

70

wondered if marrying Ben had been a serious mistake and if she would be walking in the dead woman's shadow. After all, in all the time Jane had been with Ben, he had not said any more about his first wife since that first evening in Chicago. Jane had no idea how Ben's first wife had died and she wondered, especially since Luanne was the same age as Jane was now when she died.

In the kitchen, Jane opened the refrigerator door and took the ice trays out of the freezer section. Unconsciously, she lifted the metal handle on one of the ice cube trays and popped the ice cubes out. After she had released the ice cubes from all four of the metal trays, she placed the ice cubes in clean cotton dishtowels and placed them in the box of meat.

"Ready?" Benjamin was in the kitchen holding a bulging duffle bag and looking happy. "We have to drop off the rental car on our way to the marina, Jane."

"Okay."

Dark storm clouds were rolling over the Lake when Ben and Jane arrived at the marina late that afternoon. Ben's cabin cruiser had been taken out of storage and was made ready as requested by Ben.

"Jiggs!" Ben called out as he opened Jane's door. Jiggs Boggs was at the door of his office when the couple drove into the marina's yard and came right over to the car.

"How are you, Doc?" Jiggs said as he extended his hand.

"Good, Jiggs, thank you. And how are you and your family?" Ben asked as the two shook hands.

"Good thanks, for a while I wasn't sure if you were going to be here for the Fourth. Your boat's all ready."

"Thanks, Jiggs, I appreciate it." Jane was silent as she stood next to Benjamin. "Jiggs I'd like you to meet my wife, Jane. Jane, this is Jiggs Boggs."

Jane smiled as she shook hands with Jiggs. "Nice to meet you, Jane."

"Thank you, same here," she said.

71

Benjamin looked up at the sky, "I think we need to be on our way, looks like rain."

"It's supposed to rain tonight, and tomorrow morning, but clear up by early afternoon," Jiggs volunteered.

Benjamin and Jane quickly loaded up the boat and were soon motoring on Lake Ontario. It became a long boat ride by the time they reached a small wooden dock that appeared to be anchored to a tiny spit of land inside a little cove on the spacious lake. Ben expertly lined the boat up to the dock and secured it.

"Was this your first trip on a motor boat, Jane?"

"Yes."

"What did you think?"

"It was nice. I enjoyed the ride."

"Good, I thought we could get in some fishing before dark.", Looking at the darkening sky, Ben said, "But, we don't want to be caught in a torrential rain."

"I think we are going to have to fry something for supper or eat cold meat sandwiches. We won't have time to get the charcoal burner going to grill supper." No sooner had he finished speaking than big drops of rain began to fall. "Come on, Jane, we need to go below."

Once they stepped down into the cozy cabin, Ben closed the cabin door behind them. The small windows in the cabin were covered. Jane pulled apart the curtains covering the four little windows in the cabin, letting in the day's fading light.

Benjamin was looking into the small icebox. "How about we have sandwiches?"

"That's fine with me, Ben."

"Good." He pulled the packages of meat out of the icebox and took out paper plates and cups from the small cabinet above the little stove.

Gesturing towards the stove, icebox, sink and the table and two benches in the small area, Benjamin said, "This is called a galley."

"Do I need to know boating terms?" she asked.

"It would be nice if you did," he answered with a smile.

Having a good selection of food, drink, and bakery goods on the table, the couple ate. Overhead the lit oil lamp moved gently with the swaying of the boat while creating a warm glow in the cabin. Outside the wind was sweeping across the lake. The sound of water lapping against the wooden dock and the boat were soothing. Suddenly, Jane realized the questionable thoughts that had disturbed her had receded, as Ben's appeal grew stronger.

After the table was cleared and everything put away, Ben moved over to the made up bed and lifted up the pillows. Under each pillow was a clean beach towel. Putting the folded towels on the table he turned to Jane. "Honey, take your clothes off and leave them on the table and I'll put our clothes away. We can't leave clothes, shoes or anything on the floor or anywhere else, you can get badly hurt if you trip on anything. We have one beach towel each," he added pointing to the towels.

Ben's undressing was a signal to Jane. Soon they were both naked. Jane quickly wrapped her beach towel around her to Ben's amusement as he picked up their clothes and shoes and put them away and out of sight.

"Now Jane, you need to get into bed so I can put out the lamp. It's going to be very dark in here. And you don't want to stumble."

Chapter 11 - An anniversary in July

Contented, Benjamin sighed deeply as he rolled over on to his back. He felt drained. His body was cooling down from the intense passionate heat he had felt from their lovemaking. He slipped an arm under Jane's bare back and pulled her up close to him and kissed her.

"This was the best I've ever had, Jane. You are wonderful."

"Compliment accepted," she murmured as she laid her arm over his bare chest and kissed him squarely on the lips.

"That's not an empty compliment, Jane, it's true. You are very satisfying."

Jane did not know what prompted her to suddenly question Benjamin. "Surely your first wife satisfied you?"

Benjamin had been gently stroking Jane's long soft hair when she asked that question. His hand stopped. He turned abruptly on his side to face her. "Luanne wasn't very interested in sex. She was raised in a different era than you. It was an era when nice ladies weren't supposed to be interested in sexual intimacy."

Jane had managed to keep the confused thinking that had come about when she compared the words on the mausoleum to those engraved on her wedding band, at bay. Now those disturbing thoughts were haunting her as she considered his answer to be judgmental, critical, condemning.

In the dark Ben could not see the hurt expression on Jane's face but he could hear the sarcasm in her voice as she said. "No wonder you have no children. Apparently both you and your wife flunked basic biology. It takes a man and a woman to cooperate in intercourse in order to conceive and have children, for your information, Dr. Bradley!"

Jane had slowly moved away from Bradley as she verbally lashed him. She assumed Ben was comparing his two wives. And in her mind the prissy Luanne was a princess while she, Jane, was a piece of trash. Suddenly, being on a boat on a stormy night and naked had all the unpleasant feelings of being trapped.

"That was a crude and unnecessary remark, Jane," Benjamin argued.

"Then why, Benjamin, did you stop at her mausoleum and put yellow roses there today, hours before we left on the last leg of our honeymoon? I think you're comparing me to her and my guess is I've ended up on the short end of the stick!" Feeling around on the bed, Jane found the beach towel she had wrapped around her before going to bed and now clung to it.

Trying to control his irritation, Benjamin said, "First, I am not comparing you to Luanne. I love you, even though at the moment I am questioning why I got married again. I want you to understand she is not between you and me, and will never be between us. She's dead and we are not. And second, why were you following me?"

"I wasn't following you. I was two traffic lights behind when I saw you take a left hand turn. I wondered if something was wrong, you said you were going straight home. How did I know that maybe you weren't feeling well, or had car trouble? I didn't even know that was the road to the cemetery. When I turned off and came to the top of the rise I saw that it was a cemetery and then I saw you up ahead and that you had stopped in front a mausoleum. But you drove off before I could catch up with you, so when I was near to where you had been I noticed the yellow roses and saw the name on the mausoleum. So I just left. You must have moved right along because by the time I made it to the main road you were nowhere in sight."

"I asked the florist to put the roses there. I wanted to see that was done before I paid the bill."

Not happy with his explanation, Jane's feelings remained hurt. Still clutching the beach towel, Jane finally reached the other side of the bed. She had abandoned her husband to the opposite edge, turned her back on him and pulled the covers up around her. Silence fell between them in the dark cabin.

To his way of thinking, Benjamin had a legitimate reason for stopping at the cemetery on his way home. But at the moment he did not feel obliged to tell his bride all, and did not especially want to get in an argument with her now. He heaved a heavy sigh and decided sleep was the best thing for both of them.

Time seem to move slowly as Jane waited for Benjamin to fall asleep. She listened to the rain now pelting the boat and felt the boat's movements on the choppy waves in the rising wind. When Jane thought Ben was finally asleep, she slipped quietly out of the bed and moved slowly in the dark cabin feeling her way along the narrow space between the bed and the wall.

"Where are you going Jane?"

She froze in place. She couldn't believe he had heard her; now she was annoyed. "To the bathroom," she answered.

"Are you all right?"

"Yes, I'm fine. I'll be a bit."

"It's called a head."

"OK, I'm going to the head," she said trying not to let her tone of voice reflect her annoyance with him.

As soon as she heard him turnover she continued on to the short distance to the head and stepped inside. She wondered how long she would have to stay in the tiny bathroom until he fell asleep again. By now she was determined not to go back to bed with him, but would wait until daylight to find out where he had stashed their clothes and how she could get off the boat.

When she heard what sounded like light snoring she carefully held the latch to the door opening making it as soundless as possible. Hearing no movement from the bed, she silently edged her way to the small table and benches that were across from the bed. Jane eased onto the bench furthest away from the bed.

Despite the chill, damp air Jane was determined to spend the night at the table. Certain that Benjamin held her in low esteem, she now had made up her mind not to stay with him. In the meantime she tighten the beach towel around her and folded her arms on the table, laid her head on her arms and let silent tears flow and her regrets grow until she fell asleep. Sometime later her sleep was interrupted when she felt hands on her shoulders and heard, "Come on, Jane, it's cold. Come to bed, you can tell me in the morning what you're angry about."

With his arm around her, Benjamin silently guided Jane in the dark cabin to the bed. He held the blankets up for her so she could, without fumbling, slip into the bed.

Where Benjamin had been sleeping the bed was still warm so Jane curled up on that warm place, and left Benjamin to balance himself on the cold edge.

Chapter 12 - Fireworks on the Fourth

While it was still raining that Fourth of July morning, it was a much lighter rain than the sudden stormy downpour of the night before. Jane awoke to the smell of the makings of a serious breakfast of crisp bacon, brewing coffee, and eggs frying.

"Ben," she called softly.

"Here, Jane." Suddenly Benjamin was standing beside the bed.

"I was just wondering where you were."

"Miss me?" he asked with a smile.

"Yes, you keep me warm."

"I'm glad I am good for something. Last night I thought I was someone you could just walk away from."

"Not on a boat," she stated flatly.

Ignoring her statement and the possible underlying meaning, Benjamin extended his hand to help her out of the bed. "Why don't you get up and we'll have breakfast and then discuss our differences." Jane accepted his outstretched hand.

"Scrambled eggs are the only way to cook eggs on a boat." he said, but not as an apology, knowing she liked her eggs sunny side up, as she looked at the two heaping breakfast plates he had placed on the table.

"I don't care how they are cooked, they look good." And in the next breath she asked, "How come you're eating this morning, Ben? You usually just have toast.

"Being on the water makes me hungry."

"Thank you, Ben, for cooking."

Benjamin was slowly finishing up his coffee as he patiently waited for Jane to open the discussion on her thinking last night.

After waiting what he considered a long enough time for Jane to open up, Benjamin began with, "You know Jane, I love you, but I do think we need to come to a better understanding of things between us. Would you like the first say?"

Jane looked Benjamin straight in the eyes. "Why, Benjamin, did you want to marry me when you apparently still love your wife and I guess, are still grieving for her?"

A slight smile began to crease his face. "Are you sure that's how I feel?"

"That's what I think," Jane answered in her matter-of-fact tone of voice.

"You're wrong Jane, I don't still love Luanne. I love you and I need you to believe me. I don't compare you to her. Do you compare me to Matt what's his name?"

"His name is Matt Hunter and I don't compare you to him. You two are different men and I married the man I loved."

Benjamin was touched by her response.

Jane had emphasized her response by gesturing with her hands. It was then Benjamin noticed she was not wearing her rings. So he asked. "Jane, where are your rings?"

"I left them at home."

"Why?"

Jane was stumped for an answer to his question. She wasn't sure she should tell him the real reason she left her rings behind but rather try and come up with a believable reason. "They are beautiful rings, Benjamin, and I didn't want to lose them in the lake if we went swimming."

For a moment Benjamin stared at Jane lost in thought before asking, "And?"

"And what?" Jane asked.

"And what is the other reason?"

Jane could hardly believe her ears. She wondered how did he know? So she said, "You won't like the other reason so why don't we skip it?"

"Because whatever the reason is, it's keeping us apart. So it's important I know."

Jane had no rebuttal to his argument. She heaved a silent sigh of surrender before she spoke. "At the peak of your wife's mausoleum the words "Love is forever" are carved in stone. Those same words you had inscribed in my wedding band. It is very disconcerting to me to know you have ascribed the same words to me."

"First, let's get something straight. She is not my wife, you are. Second, I did not have those words carved on that mausoleum. Those words were on that mausoleum when I purchased it. When I bought your rings I wanted to express what I felt for you. That's why I had the jeweler inscribe 'Jane, love is forever, Ben'. There is limited room in a wedding band and that was the best I could do at the time. I wanted you to understand I will love you and no one else, forever."

Looking very skeptical, Jane asked, "Did you buy a used mausoleum for your wife?"

Grinning, Ben replied, "I've never heard of a used mausoleum, Jane. She died on one of the stormiest days in January that year. She couldn't be buried. The owner of the funeral parlor suggested that I consider buying the mausoleum that had been put in the cemetery as sort of a sample."

"Otherwise, interment would have to wait until spring. So I bought the mausoleum because I did not want to go through funeral proceedings twice.

"I had no sentiment put on that mausoleum. I was only asked for Luanne's birth date and the day she died."

"When I was in Chicago, what was on that mausoleum didn't come to my mind. When I bought your rings my mind was on you only. I was tempted to ask you to marry me that Saturday. But then I thought you would consider it too soon and you would say no to my proposal. So I waited."

"Luanne and I were married on July first. The flowers were my way of finally saying goodbye to her and those years we were married."

"By the way that cemetery is in Overlook and the house we owned was in Overlook. A year or so later after her

80

death, I sold the house in Overlook lock, stock and barrel because I had bought the land in Glenwood, in part because it was closer to Switzer where I work. So, I had the house built and when it was finished I considered the move as symbolic of my starting my life over again."

"Now as for you Jane, I do not think you are at the end of a short stick, any stick. You are very special to me. And I am in hopes we will have many, many happy years together."

Automatically, Jane's arms came together, her fingers clasped, her elbows rested on the table all together forming a pyramid as she rested her chin on her outstretched thumbs and looked at Benjamin. After a short while Jane exhaled a gentle sigh as she dropped the pyramid and said, "My feelings were hurt. I guess that means I love you, Ben."

That evening Benjamin and Jane made themselves comfortable on the bow of the boat as they watched the pinwheel spin in the summer breeze and enjoyed the spectacular Fourth of July fireworks.

Chapter 13 - Monday, July 14, 1958
Orientation Day

When Jane stepped into their bathroom, Benjamin was shaving. She stood in front of the long, wide and high mirror behind the lengthy double sink bathroom vanity. Ben watched her in the mirror, wind her long dark hair on top of her head, and carefully pin it in place and then apply her lipstick.

Stepping back from the vanity , she turned to the right and to the left in her white squared toe high heels. Seeing that her full-skirted white uniform looked just right she appeared satisfied with her appearance. "How do I look, Ben?"

"Lovely, sweetheart."

"Thank you."

"Are you almost done?" Jane asked.

"Yup."

:I'll make our coffee. Do you want some toast?"

"That will be fine, Jane."

"Okay, I'll see you in the kitchen, then."

Ben was ready to go back to his practice and his position as Hospital Administrator the second week of July. The weeks away from his responsibilities had done him much good. People noticed Benjamin seemed happier, his step seemed lighter, and he didn't linger at the hospital after his day was done, as had become his custom over the years, and he did not mention to anyone at the hospital he had married again.

At the kitchen table, Ben looked a little closer at Jane. "You look a little pale Jane, are you feeling all right?"

She nodded her head. "I'm just a little nervous. I always am when I start something new."

"You'll be fine Jane, don't worry." He tried to reassure her.

Ben parked the car in his reserved space at the hospital. Ben and Jane had driven in comfortable silence the short time it took to make their way to the hospital. From time to time, Ben looked over at his wife and saw she was frequently yawning. When he opened the door for her he said, "Maybe we ought to go to bed earlier tonight." She shook her head yes as she tried to smile and stifle a yawn at the same time. "Maybe we should eat a big lunch and have a light dinner tonight," Ben also suggested.

They had entered the hallway by the back entrance of Switzer General Hospital when Jane spoke.

"A big lunch sounds fine and a light dinner maybe, we'll see. Going to bed early, however, does appeal. I don't understand why I'm so tired."

"Maybe it's because we didn't have any regimen to follow for more than five weeks,." Benjamin suggested.

"But you don't seem to be very tired, Ben."

"I've had a week to get oriented again. You'll be fine once you get use to a schedule again."

As they reached the elevators Ben said, "I have to go to both of my offices first before orientation starts. Do you have your instruction letter?"

"Yes."

"You have to go to the basement level to the personnel office first to get your packet, then to the fifth floor to the doctors' conference and lounge rooms. There should be fresh-brewed coffee in the conference room so make yourself comfortable until we get started. I think the Classroom is where they will start. Dr. Seward handles those details. Okay?"

"I'll be fine Ben, don't worry about me," she said as Ben helped her into her lab coat. "Now don't forget your promise, Ben."

"I won't, but I think we are going to find it will be difficult to keep."

"We'll see." She smiled and said, "I'll see you later." and pushed the button in the elevator.

It was easy enough to find the personnel office. Dressed in identical long white lab coats were first year interns and first year residents. They were being directed to form two lines. One of the women ushering the interns and residents turned just in time to see Jane standing outside the two lines.

Looking at Jane the woman asked, "Are you an intern or resident?

"Resident," Jane answered with a smile.

"Aha!" the woman exclaimed. "Of course, you're Dr. Jane Potts in Pediatrics."

"Yes," Jane answered ," the woman said., "You're the only woman in Pediatrics. In fact we don't have any other women in the first year Intern or resident programs except you this year. Maybe there are some in the Overlook Memorial Hospital. We won't get the names of their interns and residents until tomorrow. They're slow about giving us names and stats because rotation won't begin until January."

"That seems reasonable," Jane replied.

"My name is Irene, Dr. Potts. Let me get your packet then you can get a head start up to the Conference Room. Do you know where the Conference Room is?"

"Yes," Jane answered, and almost added, "My husband gave me a tour of the hospital yesterday," but caught herself just in time as she watched Irene head towards the personnel door. The thought crossed Jane's mind that Ben had been right about that promise.

Minutes later Irene squeezed past the two lines to reach Jane and hand her her packet.

"Thank you, Irene, I appreciate your help."

Jane was alone on the elevator until it stopped on the second floor. She had just finished pinning on her new name tag when the elevator door opened and a tall man dressed in a suit with a lab coat over his arm stepped into the elevator.

The gentleman smiled and said "Six, please," since Jane was blocking the panel of elevator buttons. Jane pushed the six floor button.

84

"Thank you," he said, looking at her name tag. "You are Dr. Jane Potts, one of our new pediatrics residents, right?"

Flashing her ever-ready smile, Jane said, "It's good to know you can read."

"I thought I'd better learn to read before I finished med school," he laughed.

"You headed up to the conference room?" he asked.

"Yes."

"Irene sent you up ahead of the others?"

"Yes."

"Must be there is coffee and doughnuts up there already." Glancing at his watch he said, "Good, I have time for some more coffee."

"Irene probably expects the gentlemen Interns and Residents will wolf down most of the doughnuts before you can pour your coffee. Good old Irene, she's always looking out for the underdog."

Jane grimaced. "Do I look like an underdog to you?"

"As a matter of fact you don't, but don't tell Irene I said that."

Smiling, Jane promised, "I won't."

Inside the conference room the smell of fresh-brewed coffee hung in the air.

The wide variety of doughnuts was temptingly arranged on large platters near the coffee urn.

"Coffee?" the gentleman asked.

"Yes, thank you."

Before pouring their coffee, the gentleman put on his lab coat. His name tag was visible above the breast pocket.

He handed Jane a cup of coffee before pouring a cup for himself.

"Going to indulge and have a doughnut?" he asked.

"I'm trying to decide between the fat greasy old fashioned or the cream-filled chocolate frosted one."

"Why not take both? The other residents and the interns will have them all devoured in about twenty minutes. I timed it one year."

Jane laughed as she put the fat greasy old-fashioned doughnut on the clear glass dessert plate.

"Well, if you're not going to eat that cream one, I think I will."

Jane smiled as she sat down at one of the three long conference tables.

Dr. David Morgan took a seat across from her.

"Dr. Morgan."

"That's me, at your service."

Jane had noted Dr. Morgan's service on his name tag. "Aha, I was wondering, Dr. Morgan, if a patient wanted to come to you for an exam, would you keep that visit and the results of that exam absolutely confidential?"

"I took the same Hippocratic Oath you did, Dr. Potts, so you don't have to worry. I'm guessing you are the patient. I'll keep this conversation confidential too." he promised.

"Is it possible I could see you privately at lunchtime?"

"Today?" he asked, sounding surprised.

"If it's possible," she added.

"My guess is you would rather not have my receptionist know you have an appointment with me, right?"

"Right."

"She usually has lunch in the cafeteria. How about I page you, it would be sometime after she leaves around noon. Okay?"

"You won't tell anyone? Oh, and I'd rather not miss any of my orientation."

"No, and you do not want to be late for any of the orientation proceedings else you will have to deal with Ben Bradley, he can be tough."

"How do you know he's tough?"

"He's a friend of mine. I've seen him put people on the carpet for things I considered minor. He had a third-year medical student thrown out of school for cheating on one test. Nothing gets past him."

"Guess I don't want to be on the wrong side of him."

"All right, so I'll page you at lunch time if I don't have an emergency or any of the usual change of plans. Okay?"

"Yes, thank you, Dr. Morgan."

David Morgan left the conference room while Jane polished off the greasy doughnut and finished up her coffee. Within a few minutes the conference doors were thrown wide open as interns and residents came through the opened doorway and jockeyed for position around the coffee urn and platters. According to Jane's watch the doughnuts were gone in less than twenty minutes.

A few minutes later Dr. Seward appeared and directed the group to another room.

That room was labeled 'Classroom.' There were five rows of desk chairs. Jane took the second seat in the second row nearest the door.

Dr. Steven Seward began his prepared welcoming speech by introducing himself and offering encouragement to all in the room before asking the young doctors to open their packets and look over their syllabi.

After a few minutes Dr. Seward asked if there were any questions. Hearing none, he suggested they review their personnel paper work first to see if everything was in order, and to correct any mistakes. As the interns and residents began this first phase of their orientation the classroom door opened and in walked the tall distinguished-looking Dr. Benjamin Franklin Bradley.

Dr. Bradley glanced around the room, his eyes rested briefly on the bent head of the resident sitting in the second seat of the second row nearest the door. On finding his wife he smiled to himself, but said nothing to his colleague, Dr. Seward.

Looking around the classroom Dr. Seward decided everyone was done with their first assignment so he called for their attention. He began, "I would like to introduce you to Switzer's Administrator and Chairman of the Intern and Residents programs here, Dr. Benjamin Franklin Bradley."

"Thank you, Dr. Seward. I personally want to congratulate all of you for obtaining a position in our Internship or Residency programs. We have some strict rules and we expect all of you to adhere to those rules. They are clearly printed out for you. You need to read them and sign the second page of the rules that states you understand them. If you will do that now."

Seeing everyone was finished, Dr. Bradley continued. "You'll notice there are several pages clipped together. I believe there are twelve in all. It is important that you read every question on those pages and answer them. When you are finished we will collect all twelve pages and the sheet listing the rules you signed. Later you will be given back all of your papers except the signed sheet of rules."

"I would like to repeat what you have heard and read about our programs here. We do some things a little differently than other teaching hospitals do. It's possible we ask more of our interns and residents than other hospitals. However, if you pass all of our requirements we believe you will be very well qualified to practice medicine in part because of the training you received here."

"Now if you will get started on those twelve pages."

Folding his arms across his chest, Dr. Bradley leaned against the standard desk in the front of the room. Behind him Dr. Seward proceeded to write the order in which they would tour the different departments and floors in the hospital, on the blackboard. First on the list was the morgue.

Except for the sound of chalk moving across the blackboard, the room was very quiet. Bradley's eyes slowly moved from doctor to doctor. As he was scanning, a flying object suddenly caught his attention. A wad of paper from about the middle of the room was heading towards the second row, second desk chair nearest the door.

Quickly and silently Bradley snatched the crumpled piece of paper in mid-air before Jane was aware she had airmail, and slipped it into his pocket. Without a word Bradley went back to observing the young doctors.

When it appeared that everyone had completed the twelve pages. Dr. Seward said. "Leave your papers on the desk, all except your list of the rules and regulations and your syllabi. We will now proceed to the morgue."

The thought of going to the morgue made Jane's stomach turn;, she was already regretting eating the greasy doughnut and she feared the sharp odor of formaldehyde would make her sicker than she already felt.

Benjamin had agreed not to treat Jane any differently than any other resident or allow her special privileges. But as Jane moved with her new classmates towards the elevators, her stomach was beginning to revolt. Looking around, she spotted Benjamin in the back of the group talking to another doctor who had just arrived. Swallowing against her stomach's rebellion, she moved quickly to the rear of the group and caught her husband's attention. He stood aside to listen to her.

In whispered tones she asked him if she could skip out on the morgue. "I get sick on the smell of formaldehyde and I ate a greasy doughnut and frankly that was not smart of me." She was hoping he would excuse her from the morgue tour.

Keeping to their prearranged agreement he shook his head no and suggested she keep up with the group. She was shocked at his response but said nothing.

The group of new interns and residents filed into and filled up all three elevators. On the trip down to the basement Jane felt squashed in the packed elevator and even queasier. Somehow, as the large group filed into the morgue, Jane ended up beside the stainless steel dissection table.

Dr. Seward introduced the Chief Pathologist, Dr. Walsh. Dr. Walsh began with, "We just finished with an

89

autopsy. Before I begin I want all of you to understand that in this hospital the morgue door is always kept locked whether we are in here or not."

"Family members have every right to expect everyone in the medical profession to be respectful of their deceased member. Remember the Golden Rule; it applies to the living and the dead in this hospital."

As Dr. Walsh went on, Jane was quickly losing the battle with her rebellious stomach. The sharp odor of formaldehyde tainted the air making matters worse until finally the time had come when Jane knew she had to bolt.

Covering her mouth with one hand, Jane pushed her way through the crowd and made it to the door only to find it locked. Panicking she brushed the door with her hands until she found the offending bolt and unlocked the door, pushed it open and rushed out.

Bradley, who was on the opposite side of the room, saw Jane bolt and followed her out of the morgue. Down the corridor he saw her push open the first door marked "Rest Room."

"Jane!" Bradley called out. By the time he reached the closed door and pushed it open, Jane was on her knees in front of the first commode and throwing up.

"Jane, this is the men's room."

"I don't care!" She yelled during a brief break from her gut-straining situation.

Finally, with Benjamin's help, Jane was able to stand up. She leaned against him for support as he guided her out of the men's room.

"I will never eat a greasy doughnut again." she declared once they were back in the corridor.

Benjamin was about to suggest something to Jane when she interrupted his thought. "I am not going into that morgue again. And furthermore, you can put a large dark check mark next to my name if you want, I don't care. I am not going in that morgue again!

Smiling, Benjamin turned her to face him. "I am not going to put any mark against your name. But I do think it's a good idea that you don't eat any greasy doughnuts." The morgue door opened and white coats began to file out and were heading their way just as Bradley bent his head down and kissed Jane on top of her head while keeping her steady with his arm around her waist.

One resident seeing the couple elbowed the resident beside him and said, "Talk about bedside manners! That old man has us beat!"

"I wonder if that's against the rules?" asked the intern walking behind the residents.

"Care to ask Dr. Bradley?" One of the grinning residents asked and added, "I hear he gives no quarter!"

"I'm going to the cafeteria, it's almost lunch time." Jane announced.

"Are you going to eat?" Ben asked.

"No, I'm going to see if there is some ginger ale or seltzer water to settle my stomach."

"Are you going to sit with me?" he asked.

"No, don't you think the people here will suspect something if I sit with you?"

"I can always say you're my girlfriend," he smiled. "And, that wouldn't be a lie, you are my wife, my girl friend and my lover all rolled into one, and I would be happy to make that announcement over the PA system."

Laughing, Jane said, "Don't you dare, otherwise I'll pretend I don't even know you."

Just as they neared the cafeteria entrance, there was a page for Dr. Benjamin Bradley. They stopped and Benjamin let go of Jane as he left her side to answer his page. Jane continued on into the cafeteria.

For a few minutes Jane had a table all to herself and her bottle of ginger ale. Soon the table was filled with residents. "How are you feeling, Jane?" a resident sitting across from her asked.

"Better, thank you."

"What's the matter?" another one asked her.

"I ate a greasy doughnut, a very big mistake on my part, and then I smelled the formaldehyde and it was all over." She said gesturing with flair. It was then she noticed she had left her rings at home.

"So you're not eating lunch?" another classmate asked.

"No, I'm just going to sip ginger ale and give my stomach a break for the rest of the day."

Sitting in the back of the cafeteria were several doctors including Benjamin. From where they sat, the doctors had the best view of the entire cafeteria.

Not long after the lunch crowd was settled in, a page for Dr. Jane Potts resonated throughout the cafeteria. Jane stood right up. "Excuse me," she said to all of them and no one in particular, just before she made a bee line to the nearest house phone.

At the back table a pair of intensely questioning eyes followed Jane as she left her table and went to answer her page. Bradley watched as she spoke for a moment then hung up and headed out of the cafeteria.

Bradley was torn between getting up and following his wife, and breaking their agreement, or sitting back and wondering about why she was paged and by whom. He reasoned if there was an emergency in her family she would have signaled him, so a family emergency was out.

Just then he remembered the crumbled paper that had taken flight and almost landed on his wife's desk. He unrolled the note, read it, then got up and walked down the aisle between the tables where the first year residents sat.

"Dr. Roger Roberts?" he inquired.

"Here, sir." A resident stood up. Bradley moved between tables until he stood across the table from the resident. He handed the note to the worried resident and said quietly, "She is not available, she is my wife."

The younger man's eyes widened with apprehension. "I'm sorry sir, I didn't know. I would never have asked if I had known she was married."

Having received the response he was looking for, Bradley was satisfied. "I know you didn't know. She doesn't want special treatment or special consideration and that's why I agreed to keep our marriage secret. Obviously that is no longer possible and maybe that's just as well."

Bradley left the young resident and the other astounded residents without another word.

Looking up, he noticed his colleagues were all looking at him and wondering what had transpired. Somewhat reluctantly Bradley walked back to his table and picked up his tray with his half-finished lunch. Internally Benjamin was smiling as he thought how Jane's plan for keeping their marriage secret had so quickly dissipated. And besides he was never in favor of keeping their marriage secret. Now he was facing his colleagues of a number of years. Still he preferred to wait and see if they would question him.

Knowing Bradley's strict attention to integrity, the established doctors at the table were all very interested in what had transpired.

"What's going on, Ben?"

"It's a private matter,." he said at first.

Eyebrows rose almost in unison, seeing the questioning looks around the table. Ben relented and said, "That gentleman asked my wife for a date. I knew he wasn't aware she is married." Grinning he added, "That's why I was easy on him."

The previous looks changed to amazement. "Who did you marry?" one friend asked. Another asked, "When did you get married?"

Jane got off at the sixth floor. She easily found Dr. Morgan's office. The waiting area of the office was empty so she went through the double doors she rightly assumed would lead to Dr. Morgan's office and his examining rooms.

"Hello!" she called out softly.

Dr. Morgan came out of his office and smiled at the young resident and said, "Hello, Dr. Potts."

Jane smiled. "Thank you for taking me during your lunch hour."

"You're welcome," David Morgan said as he escorted Jane to one of the examining rooms and handed her a jonnie and a sheet.

After the examination, Dr. Morgan said, "Go ahead, Jane, and get dressed and then we'll talk in my office."

Dressed and ready to hear, Jane sat down on the chair Morgan offered her. "Well," he began, "It looks like we'll be seeing a lot of each other for a few months."

"Yes?"

As Dr. Morgan spoke he took notes. "Although it's early, I would say the last week in February. I wrote a little book on how you need to take care of yourself. There is a section in it on typical questions and answers. Of course you can call me any time. My phone numbers are on the first page." he said as he handed the book to her.

"Thank you, Dr. Morgan."

"Now, Jane, I'd like some information for my records. So let's start with the father's name."

"Benjamin Franklin Bradley." she replied with a smile, anxious to see his expression.

"Ben, really!"

"Yes... I'm his wife." Her smile seemed brighter as she said "his wife."

"Oh, I can't wait to see him,." Morgan declared. "Let me guess, his trip to Chicago and that month plus vacation was with you?"

"Yes and see what happens when you honeymoon with him?"

"Good to know, should he ever ask me to honeymoon with him, I'll pass!" They both laughed.

"Now you will keep this visit quiet?" Jane asked.

"If I have to, but for how long?"

"I'll tell him today...Okay?"

"Then can I tease him?"

"Only if you're nice to him."

"About your bill, I understand fathers are responsible for the bills so you can give Ben the bill."

He grinned, "Medical services are free to residents and interns."

"Oh, I thought as long as we could set our own bones and stitch ourselves up that was free, everything else we paid for." she laughed.

Jane extended her hand to Morgan and smiled. "Thank you, Dr. Morgan."

"You're welcome, Dr. Jane Bradley. I will be calling you by your married name."

"That's fine. I'll have to start wearing my wedding rings all the time. Otherwise I might become the object of gossip. Besides they are too beautiful not to be worn."

. Jane was about to leave when she turned back and asked,. "Oh, by the way you said you are Ben's friend, I wonder if you knew his first wife."

A quizzed look creased Dr. Morgan's face as he answered. "Yes, I did know her. Why do you ask?"

"It's just that Ben hasn't said much about her and I wonder what she was like."

"Uhm…" Morgan seemed hesitant about answering but couldn't think of a good reason not to answer. "Ah, well my first memory of her was she was incredibly beautiful, she was a good hostess, she enjoyed throwing parties, she was very sophisticated, she was nice and that's about it. I don't know if I've satisfied your curiosity but that's really all I knew about her. You really should be asking Ben, Jane."

"I know, but I just wanted to know what an outsider thought of her. Well, you know what I mean, not really an outsider but…" she bumbled.

David Morgan smiled broadly as he put his hand on her shoulder. "Jane, I know what you mean. Don't worry about what she was like. You must be very special to Ben, and mean a great deal to him or he would never have asked you to marry him.

Jane had gotten only a few steps along the sixth floor corridor when she heard a new page. "Dr. Bradley, Dr. Jane Bradley."

Surprised, Jane looked along the walls and spotted a house phone a few feet away. "Hello, this is Dr. Jane Bradley." She answered the switchboard operator.

"Just a minute, Dr. Bradley I'll put you through."

"Thank you." she said to the operator.

"Jane where are you?" Her husband asked, sounding a bit worried.

"I'm on the sixth floor, where are you?"

"I'm in the doctor's lounge on the fifth floor; come down here."

"Am I late?"

"No, I want to see you."

"I'm coming."

Ben was waiting at the elevator when the doors open. As soon as she stepped out Ben circled her waist with his arm. "Are you all right, Jane?"

She smiled. "Yes, I have something to tell you. Can we go somewhere where we can have some privacy?"

"Yes, no one is in the lounge yet."

The Doctor's lounge in Switzer's was exceptional; its atmosphere was conducive to relaxing. There was a comfortable sofa, a couple of comfortably-stuffed lounge chairs, three four-place tables with padded barrel-back chairs. Windows looked out on a country setting, scenic peaceful paintings hung on the walls and the room even sported a piano. Just outside the glass lounge double hung doors was a wood-paneled pay telephone booth.

Ben and Jane sat close together on the sofa. "Well, where were you?"

"I was in Dr. Morgan's office." Before he could ask another question Jane announced, "Ben, we're going to have a baby the end of February."

96

"Aha, Jane." Benjamin's expression was that of a man absolutely thrilled. Speechless he took her in his arms and held her tight.

Her tears flowed freely. Ben felt those tears on his cheek. "What's the matter Jane, are you not happy about this?"

"I am, Ben. It's just I've realized how little time I have had with my mother these many years and now I need to talk to her. Can you understand, Ben?"

"I think so Jane. Do you want to call her now or tonight?"

"Maybe tonight would be better, Ben." Then she leaned against his chest. The sound of his heartbeat was reassuring and soothing. Gently he kissed the top of her head and said, "Jane, your fellow residents will be here soon. Are you going to be all right?"

"Oh yes", she assured him, as she sat up straight. "And thanks Ben."

"For what?"

"For being understanding, and for being you," she said so quietly.

"Jane, I'll be in my office on the seventh floor this afternoon. When you're done, meet me there, all right? Oh and I ordered a new name tag for you."

Jane smiled as she walked with Ben to the doorway and watched him walk down the hallway to the elevators and step into one of the elevators before she turned around and headed towards the classroom for the remaining hours given to Orientation Day.

97

Chapter 14 - September Conflicts

It was during the waning days of September 1958 when Jane's habitual inclination to leave an unhappy situation was once again aroused. Late one Thursday night Jane quietly left her marriage bed, and silently slipped into one of the twin beds in one of the spare bedrooms down the hall.

The next morning Jane was up and out of the house before Ben was awake.

If Benjamin had come looking for her during the night Jane was not aware of it.

Her feelings were hurt because of a remark he had made during a very private moment between them. For Jane it was not enough that he said he was only joking, to soothe her indignant soul.

By the time Benjamin arrived at the hospital that morning Jane was busy in the Emergency Room plastering a cast on the leg of a juvenile patient. Unknown to Jane, Benjamin had checked the ER and left after seeing her there.

Jane joined her fellow residents later that morning at one of the cafeteria tables. The quiet conversations around the table were of no great interest to her until one resident from New York City broke up the conversations by saying, "I really would like to go home this weekend but I'm on duty all weekend."

Without thinking through her decision Jane piped up, "I'll take your weekend duty, Dan if you clear it with Dr. Seward."

Looking pleasantly surprised by the offer, Dr. Dan Blake asked, "are you sure you can, Jane?"

"I'm going to need coverage in a few months so I'll take this time for you if you'll take time for me."

"You've got a deal, Jane. Thank you."

Jane's mind was on that decision as she walked out of the cafeteria with bowed head lost in thought heading for the elevators. She passed Benjamin, who was talking to David Morgan as they were going into the cafeteria, but neither Jane nor Benjamin acknowledge each other as they passed one another, surprising David Morgan who made no comment on that passing scene.

In the Doctors' Lounge a few residents and some interns were scattered around relaxing in their own way. Some had reading material in hand, a few appeared to be napping in their chairs, while a couple of them were gazing out at the peaceful country scene beyond the windows.

Jane walked in and went directly to the piano and sat down. Without a word to the others she began to softly play some slow show tunes. From time to time as she played the piano Jane would look out the windows facing the hallway and stare at the phone booth, wondering.

"Jane," one of the interns called out to her. "You're being paged." She had heard the page but hesitated to answer thinking it might be Benjamin. She was not ready to talk to him.

"Oh thank you," she said to the intern.

"Hello, this is Jane."

"Dr. Jane Bradley?" the switchboard operator asked.

"Yes."

"Will you hold for Dr. Seward?"

"Yes," Jane answered with a sigh of relief knowing the page wasn't from Ben.

"I have young Dan Blake here." To the kindly old Dr. Seward anyone less than seventy years old was young, Jane smiled to herself. "Dan says you are willing to cover for him this weekend starting this afternoon?"

"Yes, Dr. Seward, I said I would."

"Do you remember you are on next weekend?"

"Yes, I do remember. I expect I'll be needing a great deal of coverage in a few months so I am willing to cover now in exchange for coverage then."

"All right then Jane, I'll record that and I will remind young Dan he needs to cover for you when you need the coverage."

"Yes, thank you, Dr. Seward."

"You're welcome, Jane."

Minutes later the phone in the Doctors' lounge rang again. "Jane, it's for you."

The intern next to the phone held up the hand set for her. Jane was looking at some sheet music stacked on the piano when the intern called to her.

"Thank you," Jane said as she took the phone from the intern.

"Jane, I just want to thank you again for covering for me on such short notice. I'll be coming back engaged, married or dumped!" Dan Blake explained with a bit of a chuckle.

Jane laughed, "I wish you well, no matter what, Dan."

Sounding as though he was in a hurry, he ended his conversation with, "Thanks again! I'll see you Sunday."

After hanging up, Jane left the lounge and took the main stairway down to the first level floor. Outside, the balmy September breeze gently swept over her as she started to walk away from the hospital.

Jane slowly walked the entire perimeter of the hospital grounds three times.

On the last turn she was about to round a corner when she spotted the nose of Ben's car coming around. Quickly she hid behind nearby bushes and stayed there until he was well out of sight.

Feeling foolish, Jane left her hiding place and proceeded to walk in the opposite direction. Shaking her head she wondered if this time she had been too hasty in letting her feelings get between Ben and her. In her mind it was too late for her to make amends first. Her sense of pride would make it hard for her to say she was sorry. If an apology was what it would take to satisfy Ben.

It was dusk when Jane finally entered the hospital. First she checked with the switchboard operator to see if there were any calls for her. Hearing none, she wandered over to the ER. All was quiet in the ER. Lastly Jane went up to the second floor to the Pediatrics Ward. The nurses were busy feeding the children; there was nothing that needed her attention. Before she left the floor she told the charge nurse she would be in the cafeteria having dinner and afterwards she would be in the Doctors' lounge if she was needed.

Later that evening Jane wandered back down to the ER. Since it was still a quiet evening Jane went to the first room of the two rooms in the ER reserved for the covering interns and residents. She curled up on the bed nearest the door and was soon fast asleep. Sometime during the night the door to that room swung wide open and a figure looked for a moment in on the sleeping woman and then left.

The next day was uneventful. Except, it seemed strange not to see Benjamin in the hospital at all and the same was true on Sunday.

Sunday night Dan Blake looked for Jane and found her sitting alone in the cafeteria reading a magazine.

"Thanks, Jane!"

Jane looked up and flashed a smile. "Well, look who's home. So which is it? Engaged, married or dumped?"

"Engaged,." He answered with a bright smile.

"Congratulations!" she said with enthusiasm. "Now be sure you take your name off the eligible bachelors list right away!" Jane laughed.

"I will, thanks again, Jane. I really appreciate your covering for me."

"You're welcome. You look tired Dan, why don't you go home and go to bed."

"You sure you don't mind?"

"No, I'm going to bed here soon anyway and I'll take your Monday off."

101

Monday morning Jane joined the other residents in the cafeteria and waited until after eight before she finally left the hospital in search of her car in the upper parking lot. Finding it, she breathed a sigh of relief as she started it up and headed out of the lot by the back way onto a road that would eventually lead to the Ridge.

She pulled up beside the gate wishing she had the key to the gate so she could go across the field and up the trail to the top of the Ridge and become submerged in the peaceful golden beauty of early autumn. But going to the top of the Ridge was not to be.

Heaving a long sad sigh Jane admitted to herself she was still dreading facing Ben. She wished now she had called her mother. Every time she looked at the telephone booth outside the Doctors' lounge she was reminded of her mother's loving wisdom and wondered what she would advise Jane under the circumstance.

It was Monday morning and Jane was assuming Benjamin was in his office by now. So it was safe to go home, Jane thought to herself. Pulling into the garage Jane saw that Ben's car was gone.

In the house she first went into the master bedroom. The bed was unmade. Quickly she made up the bed before going into the master bathroom.

With hands on her hips Jane shook her head, wondering why Ben always seemed to miss the hamper with his laundry.

Showered and dressed in blouse and pedal pushers Jane collected all the dirty laundry and brought it down to the laundry room and started the wash.

Back upstairs Jane checked the refrigerator. Outside the golden day had turned overcast and cold. She noted she had everything she needed to make a hearty stew.

Jane spent most of the morning and part of the early afternoon finishing up the laundry and doing some light house cleaning before preparing the stew for dinner.

Once the stew could be left to simmer, Jane went back down into the laundry room and began the ironing. Doing the housework and laundry was beginning to have an invigorating, positive effect on Jane as it helped her to think beneath the surface.

The upset she had over Ben's remark now seemed to have been an overreaction on her part but she had no idea on how to rectify the situation and still keep her pride and dignity intact.

As she glided the iron over one of Benjamin's shirts she thought maybe Ben would not be happy to see her in the house, especially if now he did not consider it her home too. She was glad that she had put several clean pieces of clothing, underwear, nylons and four ironed uniforms in a paper shopping bag in the walk in closet she shared with Ben. Should she feel Ben was indifferent towards her or she felt uneasy with him she was prepared to stay away. She had no idea for how long, or if it would be forever.

She was just ironing the last article in the laundry basket when she thought she heard a noise upstairs. Glancing at her watch she was surprised to see it was just after five o'clock.

Jane feared a conflict with Benjamin. The conflict she knew was of her own doing and she had no defense for her actions. Jane would have preferred to sneak out of the house rather than listen to Benjamin's sharp reasoning.

As she unplugged the iron she was thinking she should have put the shopping bag in her car. Had she done that she could have left the house through the basement.

Packing the laundry basket with the folded clothes and the ironing on hangers on top of the basket she headed upstairs hoping for a reprieve, no matter how brief, from her crushing thoughts.

The door from the basement opened into the kitchen. A quick look around, she saw Benjamin was not in the kitchen. Putting the laundry basket in a chair she went over to the stove and stirred the stew. The tempting aroma of the stew kept her in the kitchen. But then her thoughts were back to wondering if Benjamin would tell her to leave. She tried to remember how much money she had and if it would be enough to pay for a hotel room.

Jane was so deep in thought that she was startled when she heard, "Whatever is on the stove smells good. When will it be done?"

"It's done now," she answered automatically. "Why don't you sit down Ben and I'll serve dinner."

They ate in silence. Benjamin read the evening newspaper as he ate. While Ben held up his folded newspaper and read, Jane tried to read the paper's columns from across the table.

Without warning Ben put the papers down again, startling Jane. He looked surprised. "Were you reading something?" he asked.

"Yes, but it wasn't important."

"Sorry. I was wondering if there was any more stew left."

"Yes, there is. I'll get it." Jane took his dish and filled it with a second helping.

"Thank you, Jane."

"You're welcome, Ben." The conversation between the two was brief, polite, and lacked warmth.

Jane continued to sit at the table, her mind on her next move based on her present feelings towards Benjamin. Meanwhile Ben continued to read the papers as he ate.

When finished, Benjamin lowered the newspapers and asked, "Is there any dessert?"

"No, Ben, I didn't have time to make dessert."

"It was good stew."

"I'm glad you liked it. Um, I was wondering if you..." Jane began but then decided she could not ask to sleep in one of the spare rooms, and did not finish her question.

Ben put down his papers and looked directly at Jane. "What is it, Jane?"

"Ah, nothing really Ben. I'm going to clean up now."

104

"Do you need me to leave the kitchen?" he asked.

"It's up to you," Jane answered as she began picking up. Ben remained seated and went back to reading the newspaper. In quick time the kitchen was neatly picked up, the dishes scraped and rinsed and put in the dishwasher.

Finished in the kitchen, Jane stepped behind Benjamin and over to the chair holding the basket of clean clothes. Picking up the basket she left the kitchen without a word.

After Jane had put away all the laundry she stepped back into the walk in closet and took out another one of her clean uniforms, and in her dresser she took out a slip and headed into the master bathroom.

She was out of her blouse and pedal pushers and putting on her slip just as Ben stepped into the bathroom. "What are you doing?"

Without stopping in her dressing Jane answered, "Getting dressed, what docs it look like?"

"Why?"

"Because I'm on duty tonight and I'm going to be late if I don't hurry."

"But you just covered the weekend, you have all Monday off. You can't be on tonight," he insisted.

"I covered Dan Blake's weekend, took his Monday off but now I have to cover my Monday night schedule."

"Why did you cover Blake's weekend?"

"Because I'm going to need coverage in a few months." Jane was now sounding impatient as she left the bathroom and moved into the walk in closet picking up the shopping bag she had made ready if she had decided to stay away. She decided to stay away.

Jane walked over to the bed, sat on the edge and quickly drew on her stockings, hooking them to her garter belt. Benjamin had followed her asking her questions that she, by in large, ignored as she hurried her dressing. Finally, she slipped on her shoes. She snatched up the shopping bag and headed out of the bedroom.

105

"Jane, we need to talk!" Benjamin called after her in an unusually loud tone."

"Later!" she yelled back as she opened the door to the garage, shutting it behind her.

Jane was almost an hour late as she entered Switzer Hospital but she soon fell into the hospital night shift routine. Much later that night Jane claimed the same bed she had used over the weekend and was sound asleep in minutes.

Tuesday morning was a different story. While on duty the night before there had been a rush in the Emergency Room. Jane had agreed with the intern on duty that night in the ER that some of the patients needed to be admitted; three of them were admitted to Pediatrics.

That Tuesday morning was busy for Jane and the other pediatric residents as Dr. Ralph Sawyer, Pediatrician and Instructor, made the rounds with the residents. After the rounds there was a long conference with Dr. Sawyer in the Classroom.

It was Dr. Sawyer's custom to sit down with his residents following classes at an early lunch before going back to Overlook. This was a time for questions, comments, and some camaraderie. Before Dr. Sawyer left, he would hand out a stack of papers to each student to study and be prepared to discuss the following week.

"Dr. Bradley, Dr. Jane Bradley."

Jane left the table where her fellow classmates and Dr. Sawyer sat to answer her page. "This is Jane Bradley," she said to the switchboard operator.

"Dr. Bradley, I'll connect you now."

"Thank you, Operator."

"Hello, Jane?"

"Yes."

"Hi, this is Marsha, Jane. Dr. Bradley asked me to tell you, you have an appointment with him at three this afternoon here in his Hospital Administrator's Office."

"Do you know why, Marsha?"

"I'm sorry, I don't."

"Is he in his office?"

"He's in conference now."

"Oh, all right, thank you, Marsha."

"Would you like me to call you to remind you of your appointment, Jane?"

"No, but thank you Marsha, I'll keep my eye on the time."

Jane was mystified; she had no idea why Ben had made this appointment, and that worried her.

Back at the table she smiled and acted as though the page was of no consequence.

The rest of the afternoon was busy enough to keep her mind occupied with matters other than her three o'clock appointment. It was five minutes to three when she glanced at her watch, and felt fortunate she was not in the middle of something, or a serious situation, so she could make a dash to the elevators.

Once in the elevator her mind busied itself with possible unhappy thoughts concerning this unexpected and unwelcome appointment. Jane remembered Dr. Morgan saying how tough Ben could be and how he had a third-year medical student thrown out of school. These thoughts were troubling as she wondered if Ben would use her behavior towards him in such a way to have her thrown out of this residency program.

Jane was trying to put such thoughts out of her mind when the elevator stopped and the door opened at the seventh floor. Marsha was just coming out of her office when Jane arrived.

"Oh, Jane, you are right on time," Marsha smiled. "Unfortunately your husband will be a few minutes late. He asked me to tell you to make yourself comfortable in his office. I'm going to make some coffee. Would you like some?"

"I don't think so, but, thank you Marsha."

Jane sat across from Ben's desk. She was still at a lost at what she could have done to warrant this meeting. She glance at Ben's desk it was extremely neat. His uncluttered, extraordinary neat desk was quite the contrast to his laundry around the hamper at home. She wondered if there was some underlying meaning to that.

Just as Jane was beginning to ponder that situation the door opened and in walked Benjamin.

"Jane." He nodded an acknowledgement of her.

"Benjamin." She responded like him without emotion.

Behind him Dr. Seward and Marsha stepped into his office. Marsha was carrying a pencil and a stenographer's pad.

Once Seward and Marsha took their seats Benjamin began. "If we are all set, I'll open this meeting with a question to Dr. Jane Bradley, first."

Out of the corner of Jane's eye she saw Marsha flip open her stenographer's pad and started to write. Now Jane's concerns were magnified.

Benjamin asked, "Dr. Jane Bradley, do you know why you were asked to come to this meeting?"

Jane felt very much alone when Benjamin asked that question. "No," she answered simply.

"Dr. Seward, I'll turn this meeting over to you. But first may I suggest that you explain the complaint against Dr. Jane Bradley."

"Well yes, of course," Dr. Seward agreed. "This meeting is about your covering the weekend for Dr. Dan Blake."

Jane looked puzzled but sat quietly, prepared to listen to every word before making a statement or asking a question.

Dr. Seward asked. "Did you know why Dr. Blake wanted the weekend off before you agreed to cover for him?"

"No," she answered.

"When he first mentioned he wanted the weekend off did he ask you personally?"

Again Jane answered in the negative.

"Are you saying you volunteered?"

"Yes."

"Why?" Seward persisted.

"Because, as I told you, I expect I'll need coverage for me in a few months, so I saw it as a chance to begin garnering some IOUs for that time."

"For the record, I think it would be fair to ask why Dr. Jane Bradley will need coverage in a few months, Dr. Seward," Benjamin injected.

Jane replied, "I'm pregnant. We are expecting the baby around the end of February."

"All right, did you note that Marsha?" Dr. Seward asked.

"Yes, I did."

"Good, thank you Marsha."

"Now Jane, did Dr. Blake call you shortly after talking to me?"

"Yes, he did."

"And what did he say?"

"He thanked me again for covering for him and said he would either come back engaged, married, or dumped."

"And you said what to that?" asked Dr. Seward.

"I just laughed and wished him well."

Dr. Seward looked questioning at Benjamin. "Do you have that file, Ben?"

"Marsha?" Benjamin questioned.

"That file is on your desk, Dr. Bradley."

Benjamin quickly shuffled through the neatly stacked manila folders until he picked one. He opened it and glanced at the first few pages before withdrawing one page. Without a word he handed it to Dr. Seward.

Seward looked it over then handed it to Jane and asked. "Is this your signature, Jane?"

Jane looked at the signature and glanced at the body of the page.

"Yes," she answered simply.

"Do you know what this is?"

"Yes, it's the form listing the rules and acceptable conduct for medical students, interns and residents," she answered quietly.

"As you look it over, Dr. Jane Bradley, do you see what rule concerns us in this disciplinary hearing?" Dr. Seward asked.

"I would guess it would be number five, but I don't understand why I am the subject of this disciplinary hearing."

"Because we must have two weeks notice of a change if a weekend coverage is needed. There are so many days required to fulfill the night and weekend coverage to complete the Residency program here at Switzer. We make allowances for changes in coverage in case of emergencies and very special situations. His situation did not warrant an exemption to the rules," Dr. Seward said with finality.

Jane now understood she was in serious trouble and had better think fast, or she would be forever remembered as the resident who was thrown out of Switzer's residency program, for what she considered a stupid rule. This was something she feared she could not live down, and would find it especially hard to face her parents with such a disgrace. At the moment she wished she had never heard of Switzer Hospital and had never met Benjamin Bradley.

"I beg your pardon, Dr. Seward, but since you are in charge of the scheduling you could have said no to Dr. Blake. I did tell Dr. Blake he would have to clear it with you. So, when he called me after talking to you, I thought everything was settled. The way I see it, gentlemen, I should not be the subject of this situation. You could say I'm just a bystander and none of this should reflect negatively on my record."

For a long moment time stood still. Sitting directly across from Jane, Dr. Benjamin Franklin Bradley's poker face never changed expression during this inquiry, nor during the thought-provoking stillness, as he looked directly at his wife. Dr. Steven Seward stared down at the paper in front of him during this strange moment in time, lost too in thought. Marsha had put down her stenographer's pad and folded her hands as she sat quietly, staring at the blank wall in front of her.

Finally Benjamin broke the silence. "Dr. Seward, I believe it's your call. Where does Dr. Jane Bradley stand in this?"

"I'll issue a written warning to Dr. Blake, and carefully detail a better explanation of the rule."

He went on. "Dr. Jane Bradley was correct in saying it was my responsibility to question why Dr. Blake wanted the weekend off. Therefore, I cannot hold her responsible. I will, however, issue a memo to Dr. Jane Bradley telling her to ask the need for coverage in the future, and I will work on the time off she will need prior to the birth of the baby, and following the baby's birth." Looking steadily at Jane he added with a smile, "This is the first time we've had a resident who is pregnant, so we will have to make special allowances."

"Thank you, Dr. Seward. I appreciate your thoughtfulness and your integrity," Jane said and then turned to Benjamin.

"If I am no longer needed here, Dr. Bradley, I would like to be excused."

"Thank you for your patience. You are excused, Jane."

Breathing a sigh of relief, Jane moved quickly out of the office and down the hallway into an elevator. Minutes later she was on the Pediatric floor reading the updated charts.

Hours later, Jane was in the cafeteria wolfing down a meal before rushing out of the hospital for the night. Early Wednesday morning Jane was back in the hospital showering and dressing for the day. She had managed to keep out of Benjamin's sight all that day.

After a very long and busy day Jane sunk down into a chair in the cafeteria and slowly ate her dinner.

Later, on a whim, Jane decided to do a little exploring. From the lowest level of the hospital to the top floor there was a rarely-used enclosed stairway that ran along one side of the hospital from within the hospital. The steps were made of cement and at each floor there was a small landing and a window that looked outside. An iron railing ran the entire length of the stairway along the side of the windows.

Jane mounted the stairs, curious to look out at the night from within the hospital, on the lonely stairway. At the fourth floor she sat down on the small landing and peered out at the night. At ground level, well-spaced electric lights cut a wide swath of visibility onto the driveway below that led to the reserved parking lot behind the hospital.

Looking out of the window Jane caught some movement on the driveway beneath one of the lamp posts. It was a woman in a nurse's uniform calling to someone ahead of her.

Jane couldn't hear who the woman was calling to but recognized the male figure that turned abruptly around and walked back to the waiting woman.

Jane stood up with the help of the railing to get a better look at what was going on four floors below her.

As soon as the man met up with the nurse below the lamp light, the nurse threw her arms around the man and kissed him long on the lips. Jane staggered a little at the sight, her heart beat faster and in the pit of her stomach a swarm of butterflies were beating their wings against her.

Jane gripped the railing with all of her strength as she looked down on the scene. She watched them speak briefly to each other before turning together and walking side by side towards the reserved parking lot until they were out of sight.

It was a while before Jane could muster enough strength to start back down the stairs.

There was only one thing on Jane's mind when she pulled out of the hospital's parking lot. She drove back to the Ridge where she had stayed the night before. Just past

112

the gate Jane backed her station wagon into the old forgotten road that ran beneath a canopy of low-hanging branches and parked.

Once settled in the back seat, she nestled between her two car blankets with her head on the pillow she also kept in her wagon and wondered. Had Benjamin had enough of her and found someone else? If so, then Jane thought to herself she needed to plan for a future without Ben but for the baby and herself.

Alone in the dark Jane quietly cried herself to sleep.

Early the next morning Jane awoke without a plan for the future or the day. The shock of the night before lay heavy on her. Carefully she drove out of her hideaway and headed towards Switzer where a warm shower, clean clothes and the beginning of a new day awaited.

She drove slowly, thinking as she went. Maybe it was time, Jane thought, to set Benjamin free to marry the nurse she saw him with. Jane knew she had neither the needed energy, nor know-how to try and bring him back to her.

So, rather than making more of a fool of herself, she decided to resign her position as resident and go back home. There she knew she would be welcomed. Besides, she knew the elderly doctor at home who had encouraged her to enter medicine would gladly share his office with her.

Soon after she showered and changed, she went looking for an available typewriter. In quick time she found one and soon had her resignation letter written. Next to the typewriter were paper and envelopes. She signed her letter and placed it in an envelope and brought it to Dr. Seward's office and left it for him.

That Thursday was busy enough to keep her mind off her personal life, but not enough to become overwhelmed with the duties at hand.

About two that afternoon there was a page for her. Jane answered on the first page since she was not expecting to hear from him.

113

"Jane."

"Yes, Ben."

"I have some free time at three-thirty this afternoon. I would like to talk to you."

"Where do you want me to meet you?"

"In the Conference Room."

"All right. I'll see you then," she said before hanging up.

During free moments Jane pushed hard against worrisome thoughts of her upcoming meeting with Ben. Her plans for the future were not laid out on a solid foundation. Her best hope was that Benjamin had had enough of her. And her meeting with him would not turn into a full-scale confrontation.

At three-thirty Jane opened the door to the Conference Room. Benjamin was already there. He was looking out one of the windows when Jane stepped into the large room.

Ben turned around. "Sit down, Jane. It's time we had a talk." Benjamin noticed there was no reaction from her towards him.

Sitting across from her at the table he began, "I assume you are aware that if Dr. Seward believed you had deliberately and conscientiously told Blake he could ignore that rule, or any rule, I would have been obliged to dismiss you.

"From the Residency Program?"

"Yes, and there would be no second chance of being accepted back into the Residency program here or be accepted at Overlook.

"Jane, you cannot play games with the rules and regulations. I cannot protect you if you do."

"I wasn't playing games, Benjamin. I told Dr. Seward the truth. Dan Blake did not say why he wanted the weekend off, and I do think I'm going to need coverage later on."

"There is no question Blake didn't say why he wanted the weekend off. Blake made that clear when asked. My

114

question is, what was your first reason for taking his weekend coverage?"

"I said I..."

"Jane," Benjamin interrupted and warned, "Don't lie to me. I'm asking as your husband, not as Chairman of the Residency program."

Her eyes slipped away from his face and she said nothing.

"All right," Benjamin began. "I suggest that you jumped at the opportunity to have an excuse to stay away from our home and me most of this week. Isn't that right, Jane?"

There was a long silence between them. Benjamin kept a steady eye on Jane while Jane's glance moved from place to place avoiding his look. Finally Jane spoke up. "I don't think this is the place to discuss our personal differences."

"Ordinarily I would agree with you, but you have brought this hospital and the Residency Program into our private lives, and I don't appreciate it."

"I have said absolutely nothing about our differences to anyone, Benjamin; perhaps you have and are blaming me."

"Nice try, Jane. I will not accept the responsibility for your behavior. I am not a Mr. Hyde. I have not discussed your problem with anyone!"

"My problem!" Jane sounded indignant.

Before Jane could go on the defensive, Benjamin interrupted. "It wasn't me that left our marriage bed Jane, and slept in the guest room, or volunteered to cover a weekend here so you could sleep in the hospital. And by the way, where did you sleep last night and the night before?"

"In my Woody," she answered.

"Your station wagon was nowhere on the hospital's property. Try again, Jane!" Jane had been sitting down when the argument had begun. Now she stood up. Ben was angrier than she had ever seen him before. She was worried.

115

"I parked at the Ridge," she answered.

"I have the only key to the gate to the Ridge. You could not have parked on the Ridge unless you mowed down the gate first, and I don't think you would do that."

"If you are facing the Ridge, on your left there is a heavily wooded area that looks like it goes on forever in the back, and further to the left. There looks to be what might have been a road years ago that runs beneath the trees. I parked there because I don't have a key to the gate. Otherwise I would have parked on top of the Ridge", and without thinking she added, "Where the angels fly."

That brief statement about angels softened Benjamin's anger considerably.

"Why, Jane, would you leave me to sleep in your car in the woods? I've told you I didn't get married to sleep alone and besides I shouldn't have to go looking for you at all hours of the night. In fact I'm tired of doing that."

"To answer your question, when I am upset about something I need to be away by myself and think things out, without distractions. After that remark of yours I needed to be by myself and think. Besides after what you said I thought you would prefer to have me out..."

Before Jane could finish her response, there was a knock on the Conference Room door. Ben got up from the table and answered the door. Marsha stood at the open doorway. "Excuse me, Dr. Bradley, but Dr. Seward sent these up, said you might want to see these now. He also said he'll be in his office until about four-thirty to quarter of five if you want to discuss them." Marsha held out two envelopes to Bradley.

"Thank you, Marsha."

"You're welcome, Dr. Bradley." Marsha then turned and left.

On the front of one of the envelopes was written "Rule." On the front of the other sealed envelope was the word "Advise."

Out of curiosity, Benjamin decided to read the letter with "Rule" on the envelope first. In the meantime, Jane walked over to a window, hoping the peaceful country scene outside the window would calm her inner fears.

The first letter was personal. "Ben, I have come to the conclusion that rule number five is not necessary, maybe even unjust. There are other means we can use to make sure our residents and interns fulfill their coverage time and are well-trained without burdening them or ourselves with this stringent rule. I'll explain my reasoning later. I would like to discuss this with you before I present the elimination of this rule to the board."

It was what was contained in the second envelope that brought Benjamin to the boiling point. After reading the letter in that envelope. Benjamin yelled "Jane!" as he tightly clutched the second letter he had just read.

Jane turned away from the window and walked hesitantly towards Benjamin. When she was at arm's length to him she stopped in her tracks.

"What the hell is this, Jane?" Benjamin held her resignation letter a few short inches from her face.

Jane cleared her throat and said quietly. "You read it. You know what it is. It's my resignation. I've come to the conclusion I can't be a wife and resident too. So I've decided to go back home and practice medicine as a GP."

She instinctively took a step back from Benjamin, seeing the fury reflected in his eyes. "How dare you, Jane! You are my wife! You don't just you walk out on a marriage! What's the matter with you?"

Jane was afraid. She said softly, "I have to sit down." and proceeded to move to the nearest table, pull out a chair and sit down.

Benjamin just watched her. After she was seated he pulled out a chair across the table from her and sat down. He had seen the fear in her eyes. He wished she could see and feel the breaking of his heart.

For a few minutes neither said anything. Finally, Benjamin broke the silence. "Jane, when will you understand I truly love you? We all have our feelings hurt from time to time. You shouldn't expect me to measure every word, everything I say to you, to test how you'll feel about what I'm to say. I don't expect that of you."

"We both have enough of that when we talk to our patients and their families. We shouldn't have to be constantly on alert as to what we say to each other."

He went on. "Jane, you need to grow up. Face the fact that no one is perfect, not even you. We both need a stable life and I believe we can have that..."

It was Benjamin's remark about growing up that caused Jane to snap back, interrupting him. "Having a stable life for you and me is out of the question," she said as she stood up and glared at him. "When you are already looking for wife number three!!!"

Shocked, Benjamin's eyes narrowed as he asked, "What are you talking about? I have enough trouble with you! Why would I look for more trouble?"

"Last night I saw a woman call to you in the driveway and the two of you kiss then you two went off together to who knows where and to do who knows what!"

Benjamin laughed. "Oh, that was Amy Walters. Her husband and I have been friends for years. I was his best man at their wedding. Amy sometimes works as a private nurse in this hospital and as a float. She is an excellent surgical nurse and she is good about coming in on short notice in that capacity. Nothing is or has gone on between her and me and will not," he said with finality.

"

"Why did you laugh?"

"Because up to now, I have thought you didn't give a damn about me. I'm happy to say I guess I was wrong. Am I right?"

Jane hesitated, closed her eyes and thought before answering. "There are times, Benjamin, when you say the

118

stupidest things to me. I don't think you mean to hurt my feelings, but I guess I take things to the extreme. It's always been easier for me to walk away from anything or anyone who annoyed me. It is easier for me to walk away than apologize."

"I have not forgotten I am married, or more that I am carrying your child. I thought my actions might make my life complicated, but then I thought after seeing you and that nurse kiss, I no longer had a choice but to resign and be a GP back home where I would have help raising our child."

Jane noticed the patient tone in Benjamin's voice as he asked again, "Was I wrong to think you didn't give a damn about me, or my love for you?"

"Yes, Ben."

"Now is everything settled between us?" he asked.

"I hope so," she answered and added, "I do love you, you know." Her voice was soft and apologetic.

"Good." He smiled as he tore the letter concerning her resignation up. "I'll tell Seward you aren't resigning but with the baby coming we may have to do some rescheduling of your residency obligations. Does that sound reasonable to you, Jane?"

"Yes, it does, and thank you Benjamin."

"Oh, by the way, now that we have settled things I need a date for next Saturday, care to fill in?"

"Where is this date?"

"Ah, it's under the stars and not that far away."

"Oh, I can't, Ben."

"Why?"

"I'm on duty all weekend. Darn it! A date with my husband is just what I need."

"Oh darn!" She exclaimed again as she glanced at her watch. "I have to go Ben, I'll see you tonight."

"Where are you going?" Benjamin called to her as she was almost at the door.

"I have an appointment at four."

"With whom?"

"David Morgan, it's my monthly appointment."

"When do you finish up today?"

"I'm not sure; six or seven tonight."

Ben met her at the door. He grabbed her arm and pulled her close to him and kissed her lovingly. "I missed you, Jane," he quietly admitted.

"Without you Ben, I was cold."

"That's an understatement," he grinned as she pushed the door open.

At four that afternoon Jane was David Morgan's last patient for the day.

Unheard by either doctor or patient the door to the examining room opened.

"I hate these exams, David," Jane was saying.

"Jane, I could retire early if I had a dollar every time I heard a woman tell me that. I'm being as discreet as I can."

"I know you are David. I'm just complaining, it's the only thing I seem to do well."

"Don't be so hard on yourself, Jane. Is there something you want to talk about?"

"No, but thank you, David."

"You know, you are beginning to look very tired. I'm wondering if fulfilling your duties as a resident is becoming too much."

"I rest when I can," she said as David helped her to sit up.

"I don't think that is going to be enough, Jane."

"What are you saying, David?"

"Your blood pressure is too high, you've lost some weight and I not happy about that either. So, after I see your blood work, I may tell you to put a hold on your residency aspirations."

"I can't, David!"

"Yes, you can Jane, for your sake and the baby's sake. I had a patient a few years ago in similar circumstances. She argued with me, telling me she couldn't stop the work she was doing. Both she and her baby died at my office door a few weeks later.

"I will not tolerate any argument from you. After I see the results of your lab work I'll make my decision. In the meantime be good to yourself and the baby. You need a few days of real rest, starting today."

"Excellent advice, David."

Both patient and doctor expressed surprise at seeing Benjamin coming around to the examining table. "I didn't realize you were here, Ben," Morgan stated.

"I didn't want to disturb you," Benjamin said as he stood next to the table and took Jane's hand in his hand.

"Then you heard me Ben, she needs to rest?"

"Yes I did, but she is scheduled to work tonight until six or seven and starting tomorrow cover for the whole weekend."

Even before Ben had finished with Jane's schedule David Morgan was shaking his head no.

"Ben, she needs to rest now, not next week, not next month, now," Morgan emphasized.

Ben scooped Jane up and off the table then gently helped her to stand up. "Why don't you get dressed, Jane? I'll wait for you here."

While Jane was dressing Benjamin turned to David. "I'll call Seward, tell him as her doctor you said she needs to rest now and let him find coverage for her."

"Right, it's very important that she does," Dr. Morgan stated as he turned to leave the room.

Picking up the phone, Benjamin asked the operator to page Dr. Seward and then put him through Dr. Morgan's office, and then call his office and Polly Fields.

His receptionist Polly Fields answered right away. "Polly, what do I have scheduled for tomorrow morning?"

"No surgery, your first appointment is at ten."

"Good, would you lock up when you're done? I'm going straight home."

"Is everything all right, Dr. Bradley?"

121

"I have to take my wife home and make sure she rests for the next few days."

"If there is anything I can do, let me know, Dr. Bradley."

"Thank you, Polly."

Right after Ben hung up with Polly the phone rang. "You caught me just as I was about to leave, Ben. What can I do for you?"

"David Morgan has ordered a few days of rest for my wife, starting now. So will you get one of the residents to cover for her starting now until six or seven tonight and tell Dan Blake he has to cover the weekend for her. We'll see how she is on Monday; she may have to stay out longer."

"And her resignation?" Seward ventured to ask.

"It's about rescheduling not resignation."

"Oh good, she is highly respected in her residency. I hope she'll finish."

"Right now we have to concern ourselves with her health and the baby's health."

"I understand Ben. Tell her not to worry; I'll take care of her coverage. I hope they both will be fine."

"Thank you, Steven."

Just as Ben hung up the telephone Jane stepped out of the dressing area. "Are you ready, Jane, we're going home."

Jane smiled and shook her head "I can't, Ben. I have to cover tonight until six or seven," she said as Ben circled her waist with his arm.

"No Jane, you'll be covered for tonight and for the next few days. You are going home and rest for your sake and the baby's sake."

Once Jane was in Benjamin's car she began to relax. "You know, Ben, I didn't realize how tired I've been until now. My every muscle is aching. You would have thought I have been shoveling manure all day." She yawned and smiled at the same time.

"You've been running on adrenalin for most of the week, and now you're out of fuel. Rest for a few days and you'll be fine," he assured her.

"What about this Saturday date?"

"There are two Abbott and Costello films playing at the drive-in on Saturday. "Abbott and Costello meet Dr. Jekyll and Mr. Hyde" and the other one is "Abbott and Costello meet the Mummy.""

"Those movies have been out a few years but I haven't had a chance to see them. So, do I have a date?"

"Well," she began in a sly voice, "Do I get a box of hot buttered pop corn if I go with you?"

"It's a deal," he promised.

"Ah not so fast Benjamin, one more thing."

"Yes?"

"No more of this kissing Amy business."

Chapter 15 - A Reunion in December

Just as Benjamin and Jane sat down for dinner the phone rang. "Do we toss a coin to see who is going to answer that?" Jane asked.

"No, I'll get it," Ben answered as he moved out of his chair. "You aren't on call, are you?" He asked with a frown.

"No," Jane said.

"I didn't think so," he mumbled as he reached for the telephone.

Before she could ask him the same question he had picked up the telephone hand set. "Dr. Bradley."

At the sound of the voice at the other end of the wire Benjamin's face broke into a broad smile. "Alex, how are you?" Then in a more somber tone he asked the caller, "Everything all right?"

"Everything is fine," the caller reassured Benjamin. "How are you?"

"Good, Alex. Thanks."

"Have some time to talk now?"

"Sure, my wife and I were just sitting down to dinner. But that's okay."

"Did you say your wife, Ben?"

"Yes, Jane and I were married in June."

"Well, that's quite a bit of news. You can be sure the girls will be chewing on that fat for a while." He chuckled. "How come we didn't get an invitation?"

"Because it was a private ceremony with a couple of witnesses we didn't know and a judge who officiated, nothing fancy. So what's new with you?"

"Nothing as interesting as you! What I called about is some of us thought why not have a private reunion, you know Mac, Simon, Henry, Tim, George, you and me the old gang, the seven musketeers." Benjamin smiled broadly as he pictured the old gang as they were as young medical students.

124

"Sounds good, where and when?"

"Here in Philadelphia, how about being here Sunday, December 21. Okay?"

"That should be fine. I'll book a room at the Philadelphia Regency for Jane and me."

"Great, I'll tell everybody you're coming. Call me when you book your reservations so I can meet you when you get into town."

"All right, will do."

Back at the dinner table Ben answered Jane's inquisitive look with, "We've been invited to a reunion in Philadelphia December 21 for a couple of days, I think."

"You think? Are we going to be home for Christmas?"

"I'm sure we can be."

"You didn't ask, did you?"

"No, I forgot."

"Okay, let's try a simpler question. Do you know who these people are, asking for this reunion?" She asked in a facetious tone.

"Yes, of course, they are six of my classmates from medical school. Alex who called has been a friend of mine since our high school days."

"I'll have to ask Dr. Seward if I can have a few more days off so I can go."

"No. I'll tell him you are taking time off. You're going to have to make up your time off after the baby is born before you can complete your residency anyway, so it's better I tell him."

Jane didn't understand Benjamin's reasoning on the matter but was willing to accept his willingness to talk to Dr. Seward on her behalf.

It was a pleasant surprise to see Alex Martin waiting at the airport when Benjamin and Jane arrived. It was obvious the two old friends were genuinely happy to see each other as they shook hands and clapped each other on the back as they exchanged greetings. Jane smiled as she watched the two men.

Benjamin turned towards Jane. "Alex I'd like you to meet my wife, Jane."

Alex extended his hand to Jane with a big handsome smile that hid his thoughts concerning Ben's young-looking wife. "It's nice to meet you, Jane," he said as the two shook hands. Like Benjamin had noticed when he first met her; Alex observed Jane's handshake was firm and sure.

"Thank you and the same here, Alex. Ben has told me about some of your antics back when you two were in medical school and as interns. I gathered of the two types of humor preferred by some of the interns and residents, the macabre or humor a washed in sex, apparently you two preferred the macabre. I think you both should be ashamed for putting those corpses on the x-ray tables and scaring the x-ray technicians," Jane smiled.

"We were both too dumb to be ashamed of ourselves then and I think we both are still too dumb to be ashamed of ourselves now," Alex's replied with a big grin.

"Jane, why don't you wait here while I get our luggage then we can be on our way," Ben suggested.

"If you'll be all right Jane, I'll go help Ben," Alex offered.

"I'll be fine, you two go ahead."

Out of earshot, Alex said with a smile, "I see you've been busy, Ben. When is the baby due?"

Beaming. Ben answered, "The last week in February."

"So you're going to have a baby after all! Long in coming but well worth the wait, right?"

"Right!"

"You know Ben, I've thought about this over the years, even knowing you wanted children, but I don't think Luanne would have made a good mother."

Ben responded abruptly. "We aren't going to talk about her, are we?"

"No, sorry if that upsets you," Alex apologized.

126

"It's not that. I don't want Jane upset. Whenever Luanne is mentioned Jane seems to become less confident about herself. I don't want her to feel that way. So the less talk about Luanne the better for Jane."

"I'll remember that, Ben."

"Thanks, Alex."

In the front of Alex's car the two friends gabbed away like a couple of old ladies at a card party. Jane considered herself fortunate to be in the back seat to view the Philadelphia scenery uninterrupted.

"Ben, I was wondering if you would assist me in surgery tomorrow morning?" Alex asked.

"Be happy to, what time?"

"Be ready to scrub at seven."

"I'll be there."

The next morning while Bradley was scrubbing up Dr. Alex Martin was aside talking quietly to one of the nurses. When he finished talking he handed her a piece of paper and said thank you as the nurse turned to leave the room.

The surgical team was about a half-hour into the bowel resection when the nurse he had spoken to came into the operating room and nodded towards Alex. A few minutes later an obviously pregnant woman small of stature dressed in surgical scrubs stepped into the operating room, walked over and stood by Benjamin. Benjamin immediately recognized his Jane.

As the chatter in the operating room began to slow down with the new arrival Bradley said in a lukewarm tone, "Good Morning, Sunshine."

"Good Morning," Jane responded with little enthusiasm.

"So, what were you reading last night, War and Peace?" Ben asked quietly.

"No I've already read that. I was reading one of Agatha Christie's mysteries," she answered flatly.

Then he asked, "So when did you come to bed?"

Jane was surprised at Benjamin's questioning her in front of strangers and was beginning to resent it. "About an hour before you got up," she stated as a cold matter of fact.

The normal chatter around the operating table resumed when everyone realized conversation between the two had ended.

It was a long while before Jane spoke again and when she did she asked, "Will my being here qualify me for the required CD time in the OR?"

To the surprise of the surgical team Benjamin responded with a question in a cold, sarcastic tone.

"Is this Switzer?"

"No," she answered.

"Then the answer to your question is no."

Before Jane could respond Alex jumped into the conversation by asking. "What's this required CD business, Ben?"

"Civil Defense wants hospital staffs to be able to respond quickly and efficiently should a major disaster occur in the area. So we have to have practice sessions on every shift with every department responding."

"How are they going?"

"They aren't. I'm working on a triage strategy that is suitable for a hospital that may be confronted with a multitude of different emergencies all at once, before we start practicing."

Jane was grateful to hear Alex asking questions about the Civil Defense requests. She hoped he would keep Ben's thinking busy enough so that he would not needle her any more. It was becoming apparent that Benjamin was still unhappy with her for not going to bed when he did last night.

"Haven't you been approached by the Civil Defense Division here?" Bradley asked.

"I don't know, it's up to the Hospital Administrator to tell us about applicable policies and he hasn't done that yet."

128

"I expect you'll receive some notice in the near future," Ben suggested. "I think they are still concerned about atomic blasts, but then, who knows for sure!"

"Oh, by the way everyone, the young lady standing next to Benjamin Bradley is Jane Bradley, Ben's wife," Alex finally announced.

One of the nurses asked Jane, "Are you a nurse, Jane?"

"I'm afraid I don't have the patience, or the wherewithal to be a good nurse; however, I've been told on good authority that by being married to a doctor that automatically makes me half doctor and three-quarters idiot!"

There was no shortage of laughter in the operating room following Jane's remark with one exception. Dr. Benjamin Franklin Bradley was not amused.

"Are you paying attention, Alex?" Benjamin asked in a sobering tone.

"Yes, I am, Ben," Alex answered in his usual easy going manner.

"Just making sure you're awake, Alex. Do you think we can be a little serious here folks?" Ben asked no one in particular.

If Alex was unhappy with the resulting strained mood he didn't say anything.

The surgical team worked in relative silence for a long while until one of the younger nurses asked if anyone had seen the latest Tarzan movie. No one responded. Then Jane said. "I saw the movie that told of Tarzan meeting Jane. I don't know how recent that was."

"How was it?" the young nurse asked.

"It was okay," Jane began. "The most interesting thing was Tarzan's home. It looked like an enormous bird's nest propped up on its side situated high up in a tree with a gorilla guarding the entrance."

"The scenery was pretty good. I like adventure stories in faraway places but I just can't get enthusiastic over a man swinging through the trees in a loin cloth!

"However, since I haven't had any coffee yet, if Tarzan should show up here swinging on a vine in his loin cloth, and asked me to join him for coffee, I wouldn't think twice, I'd go!" The resulting chuckling was somewhat contained.

"Jane." Benjamin's stern tone was a warning for Jane to stop.

An older nurse spoke up and said, "For my money I'd take John Wayne over Tarzan!"

Jane jumped in with a laugh. "There is nothing like a man in a Cavalry uniform rushing off on his trusty steed to save the West. You could almost swoon!" She grinned. There was more giggling and grinning from the surgical personnel following those remarks.

Slowly and quietly Jane inched away from Ben's side while Benjamin, Alex and their mutual friend and fellow musketeer Timothy Wang, the quiet anesthesiologist, talked about the patient's progress.

The doctors agreed the surgery was a success and the patient was doing well. Then without warning Alex asked Benjamin. "Ben, will you close for me?"

"Sure," Ben responded.

In the next breath Alex motioned to Jane as he yanked off his blood-stained gloves, "Come on, Jane. I have a vine just waiting to take us to the coffee shop downstairs."

Alex took Jane by her upper arm before she could respond to him, and led her out of surgery through the scrub room down the corridor and into the surgical waiting room. "Mrs. Carson," he addressed the patient's wife, "Your husband came through fine. He will be in recovery for a while then we'll bring him to his room."

A look of relief flooded the middle-aged woman's face when she heard the good news. Her adolescent children's faces reflected the same feelings as they politely listened. "It will be a while before you can see him so you have time to relax."

"Thank you, Dr. Martin." Mrs. Carson smiled.

"You're welcome, Mrs. Carson, I'm glad we could help your husband. We'll see you later," he said as he escorted Jane out of the surgical waiting room.

"Okay, Jane," Alex sighed as they headed toward the elevator. "No doubt Mrs. Carson is wondering who you are, so I'll tell her and my surgical staff as soon as I find out."

Jane looked at him in stunned silence. In the coffee shop, Alex asked Jane if she wanted something to eat with her coffee. She shook her head no.

They found a small table at the far end of the room and settled down with their coffee. Jane sat quietly waiting for Alex to explain himself.

After a few sips of coffee Alex began. "I know, Jane, you are married to Ben, and that you are carrying his long-awaited baby, but I know something about you that you and he are keeping secret and I want to know why."

The expression on Jane's face showed she had no idea what Alex was talking about. Alex correctly read her expression and went on to explain.

"On a hunch, last evening I called Switzer General Hospital and asked for Jane Bradley. The switchboard operator said and I quote: "I'm sorry but Dr. Bradley is not on this evening."

"And so, I said I'm not looking for Dr. Benjamin Bradley, I'm looking for Jane Bradley. The operator said, "But sir, I was referring to Dr. Jane Bradley, Dr. Benjamin Bradley's wife." Then I asked what practice is she in and the operator said she is a Pediatric Resident. And then the operator said, "I'm sorry sir but that's all the information I can give you." So I thanked her and hung up.

"Now my question to you is: why are you and Ben trying to hide the fact you are a doctor?"

"Well, you see Alex, I like being a feminine female and I'm not giving that up even though I am a doctor. Socially, however, some women don't accept me as one of the girls, and frankly I miss that. So I said to Ben, since this was a social event I don't want the other wives to know I'm a doctor."

"It's pretty obvious I am pregnant, and I imagine the other ladies will probably have something to say about their pregnancies and deliveries and raising their children. I want to hear what they have to say. Yet, if they find out I'm a doctor they might think I know every intricacy of being pregnant and being a mother. I don't want them to feel intimidated by me, and be so uncomfortable with me that they will say nothing to me."

"Besides I like being married to Ben and having his baby. Being away from the medical profession I can indulge in the nice thing it is to be a wife and mother. So there is no real mystery, Alex." She smiled and asked, "Now is that why you asked a nurse to call me to come this morning, to see if I would reveal my being a doctor in the operating room?"

Alex smiled warmly, "Something like that," he admitted. "I'm glad you came, Jane, you are special, Ben is fortunate, hope he appreciates you.
"I know Ben runs his operating room different than I do. I don't mind most chatter when I operate. It's not distracting for me. Ben is just the opposite. He wants it quiet in his operating rooms with only necessary conversations accepted. But then I have better bedside manners than he does!" He accented that statement with his handsome smile.

But then Alex quickly looked serious. "Ben did take me by surprise when he snapped at you."

"Ben likes me to go to bed when he goes to bed. Since I can be very obstinate, and I am very independent, something he hasn't gotten use to yet, sometimes he has to say something unexpected to get my attention. I bought two books before we boarded the plane yesterday. Reading fiction is very relaxing for me. I had planned on reading one of the books while we were flying. Ben, however, was

132

in a chatty mood so I never got around to cracking open one of those books until he went to bed last night.

"Needless to say, he was not overly happy when I started to read because I tend to get lost in whatever I'm reading and don't always hear anything."

"So he was probably asking you to come to bed and you just read on and didn't hear him," Alex suggested.

"That's not the first time that has happened. He'll get over it. Although, he doesn't usually make any snappy remarks to me in public." She continued, "As long as he doesn't make a habit of making smart remarks to me especially in public, then we should live happily ever after," she smiled.

Just then Benjamin joined them.

"Is the patient in recovery, Ben?"

"Yes, Alex, and he is stable."

"Good, thank you."

"Any time, Alex. By the way, what time is dinner?"

"Cocktails at six, dinner at seven. It will be held in one of the private dining rooms in your hotel. We couldn't have made things more convenient."

"We appreciate that, Alex."

"So what are you two going to do today?"

Ben answered. "Jane needs to shop for a gown; we will be attending the New Year's Eve Ball in Overlook. Besides, we don't want to spend Christmas in a hotel. So we need to be ready to leave tomorrow morning."

"Can't blame you for not wanting to spend Christmas in a hotel; you're welcome to join Janice and me and our family for Christmas." Alex offered.

"Thanks Alex, but we should be able to be back home tomorrow. Next time you musketeers decide to hold a reunion, try holding it in the summer."

"Will do," Alex responded as he rose from the table. "Okay, we'll see you tonight. Do you want me to send the waitress over?"

"I just want coffee. Do you want anything, Jane?" Ben asked.

"Not for me, thank you."

Having received his answer Alex left the couple. Ben leaned across the table and began to speak in a very quiet voice.

Jane had an idea what was coming and wished she could just get up and leave.

"Jane, I take medicine very seriously and just as seriously surgery. I do not like disruptions in the operating room, antics of any sort. I would not have allowed the conversations that you engaged in during surgery. It's distracting and improper given the arena. I will not tolerate it in the Switzer's Operating Rooms. I'm giving you fair warning because you will be assigned surgery assistance with me."

"Ben, you know I don't like surgery and I would not like being asked to assist in surgery with you, or anyone else."

"You don't have a choice, Jane. The Civil Defense program will be instituted in less than a month's time and you had better be ready for that."

Ben leaned back in his chair as a waitress brought him a cup of coffee. "Your coffee is on Dr. Martin." the waitress said. "Thank you," Ben smiled as he spoke to the waitress.

Jane had no response for Benjamin. The pleasantries she had just exchanged with Alex were swept away with Ben's unforgiving lecture and the unwanted news she would be assisting him in surgery. She sighed and wished again she could be gone from there. Now Jane desperately wanted to be home on the farm celebrating Christmas with her family. She began to think it would be a very long day and night for her.

To Jane's surprise, dinner with Ben's friends and their wives turned out to be a very pleasant experience. Alex's wife Janice was particularly interested in making Jane feel welcomed in the group.

After dinner the men mounted the bar stools nearby, while the women remained at the dinner table. Jane had excused herself to go to the ladies' room earlier.

On the way back she walked very near the far end of the bar. Benjamin had had a couple of drinks before dinner. Jane thought Benjamin knew how much alcohol he could tolerate, she wasn't concerned. But Ben was at the far end of the bar and when he saw her coming, he spun around on the bar stool with a drink in his hand. It was evident Benjamin was intoxicated when he grabbed her hand and pulled her over to him. "Have a book you need to read tonight, Jane?"

At first Jane said nothing and tried discreetly to pull her hand away, but he held her steady and asked again, "Well, do you?"

"No," she said quietly. Looking around it appeared that the men had spread themselves around the small temporary bar and no one seemed to be paying attention to Benjamin and Jane.

"Smart," he said and tipped his glass towards her and then finished his drink. Benjamin released her hand and she immediately turned away from him. She wasn't sure if anyone had heard or seen Benjamin's drunken reaction to her. She did know she was embarrassed for both of them and needed to get away.

Jane walked over to the table where the other wives were. She stood by the table and said quietly, "It was very nice meeting all of you. And I want to wish all of you and yours a very Merry Christmas and a bright New Year."

"If you'll excuse me I am very tired and I need to go to bed. Good night ladies."

Janice Martin stood up and said, "Jane, let me walk you out."

Jane preferred to walk alone to think without distractions about her latest decision, but that was not to be.

As Janice and Jane left the private dining room Jane asked, "Did you know Ben's first wife?"

"Yes, Jane, I did."

"What was she like?"

"Listen, Jane, Ben loves you. Don't dwell on what his first wife was like." Janice's reassuring smile was sincere.

"I'm just curious, Janice."

"Well, the one thing that stands out in my memory of her was that she was incredibly beautiful. Luanne always turned heads and she enjoyed that. She was more beautiful than most movie stars. She wore just lipstick; no pancake makeup for Luanne! She was attractively slim and tall."

"What about her personality?" Jane pushed.

"She was nice, a very gracious hostess, polished, a sophisticated lady." Janice looked at Jane and said, "In many ways you are not like her and that's good."

"You see, Ben and my Alex were roommates in college and the best of friends years before, so naturally when Alex told me Ben had married again I've, well, been very curious. I've been observing you to see what kind of woman Ben married. In my opinion you are the better of the two."

"Why?" Jane asked.

"Because, Jane, you have a nice personality, a quick wit and Alex told me last night you're a doctor too. After talking to you this morning, Alex told me why you didn't want anyone to know. That says a lot about you and that's good. Besides Ben is thrilled he's going to be a father. And, I don't think Luanne wanted any children, in my opinion."

"Why didn't she want children?"

"She didn't come right out and say why. She just sort of hinted at times she didn't want to bother with children. She never gave any direct reasons."

"Well, he is a father already, Janice. As I reminded him, once conception has taken place the man is already a father and the woman is already a mother, they are just waiting for the baby to fully develop."

136

Janice smiled. "You know, you're right."

"Thank you, Janice, for your kindness. If you will excuse me I am very tired; I think I'll take the elevator."

"Good night, Jane. Take care."

Chapter 16 - A Journey

In their hotel room Jane made a call to an airline. She learned there were late night flights that could get her close to home and an airline that did fly into the small airport a few miles from the family farm.

She made a serious decision. One she had been mulling over since that morning in the operating room. She made a reservation. Then she wrote a poignant but brief note, one she guessed would disturb Benjamin.

Quickly she packed her suitcase and hurriedly went back down to the lobby. The doorman hailed a cab and in minutes Jane had taken the first step on her way home.

While there were a couple of plane changes, Jane didn't seem to care so long as she reached her destination. It was early morning when Jane found a cab driver that would drive the fifteen miles from the small airport to her family home at a reasonable price. Once inside the cab Jane sighed. Finally, she would be home for Christmas.

Jane quietly stepped into the Potts farm house kitchen that Tuesday morning December 23, 1958. Scooter was nowhere in sight, a mixture of memorable Christmas spices scented the kitchen air, the radio was playing Christmas music as Marjorie Potts was holding the oven door open to check on her baking.

This was the scene Jane had cherished since childhood and wanted to relive again. Marjorie did not hear her daughter close the door nor feel the winter wind briefly rush in with Jane. In silence Jane saw her mother studying whatever she was baking then shut the oven door having decided the baking was not done.

Jane's glance swept over to the table. It was laden with flour, spices, sugar, bowls, dried fruit, walnuts, pecans, and eggs, everything it took to make the most delicious of Christmas treats.

Marjorie turned away from the stove and saw to her amazement her daughter quietly standing in the kitchen. She drew her hand across her eyes. For a moment Marjorie Potts thought she was imagining things. Softly, she called "Jane." It was true; she saw her daughter's bright smile increase and heard, "Merry Christmas, Mom."

"Oh Jane!" Marjorie's eyes were welling up with long held back tears as she stretched out her arms to embrace her daughter.

It was not like Jane's mother to weep. "Oh Jane I've been thinking of you all morning. I was remembering Christmases past and when you and your brother were little." Marjorie dabbed at her eyes with the corner of her apron. "It's been so long since you've been home for Christmas. What a wonderful Christmas surprise, to have you home!"

"Sit down Jane, would you like some coffee, cookies?"

"That sounds good. I'll get them."

"No, no, sit down. Where's Ben?"

"He's in Philadelphia helping a friend and fellow surgeon."

"Will he be here for Christmas?"

"No."

"Oh that's too bad. It's sad he doesn't have any family besides you. We are hoping that Ben will consider us family. He's such a nice man."

Jane did not comment on her mother's opinion of Ben as Marjorie placed coffee and a plate of Christmas treats on the table before sitting down herself.

"Oh Jane, did you notice my electric mixer?" Her mother asked as she gestured towards the counter where the heavy duty mixer on a stand sat.

"Wow, Mom, that's nice! It looks sturdy."

"It does everything, even kneading dough. It's just wonderful; it does all the hard work in baking! Your father said I should buy one with some of the three thousand dollars you and Ben gave us."

Jane smiled. "I'm glad Mom you bought that mixer; it's just right for you. Did Dad buy anything?"

"No, he wanted to save most of the money for a rainy day but he did say he would like to go to New York when the baby is born. I know he wants to see where you and Ben live and the hospital you're doing your residency in and if we can arrange things come see you in the summer too.

"You know we haven't traveled much, and we haven't seen much of you Jane over the years and well..."

Jane reached across the table and patted her mother's hand as she interrupted her. "I understand Mom. You know you and Dad never need an excuse to come see me. My family is always welcomed to come wherever I am.

"Where's Dad now?"

"He's working in the barn."

"I think I'll change and go out and see him."

"He'll be so happy to see you, Jane. It will be a nice surprise."

"Thanks Mom." Jane said as she snatched up her suitcase and headed towards the stairway.

"Merry Christmas, Dad." Scott Potts put down his hammer and looked up from his carpentry work. Seeing his daughter, he quickly stood up and embraced her.

"How are you, Sis, what a nice surprise, you home for Christmas?'

Smiling broadly, Jane answered. "I'm fine, and yes, I'm home for Christmas."

"Where's Ben?" her father asked.

"He's in Philadelphia helping a friend and fellow surgeon."

"Will he be here for Christmas?"

"No."

140

"That's too bad. We would like him to feel like a member of our family. It would have been nice to have him see what a country Christmas is like. Well maybe next year."

"Maybe," Jane said, while in fact she was thinking not next year or any other year. She had strong doubts about returning to Benjamin after the way he spoke to her in the operating room and then his drunken words last night. While it was the first time she had ever seen Benjamin take a drink much less drunk, she would not have a drunk anywhere near their child, or her.

Before her father could ask any more questions Jane said, "I think I'll go for a little walk, Dad, I've been riding for hours."

"Are you bundled up?" Her father asked the time-honored winter's day question.

"Yes."

"Okay then, wouldn't be surprised if there will be more snow today. Take Scooter with you." Before Jane could object, her father was calling for the family dog.

"He better stay with me, Dad," she said as Scooter came from around the far corner of the barn. "I am not going to chase after him," she said with finality.

Grinning, her father said as he patted the dog's head, "Like some people, Scooter has gained wisdom with age. I bet he knows you'll leave him in the handiest snowdrift if he takes off. Remember Jane if you need help Scooter will come get us and lead us to you. So don't be so quick to dump him," Scott Potts advised.

"Don't worry Dad, I won't. It's just that he can be a pain in the neck when he sees a rabbit or a squirrel. I'm not going to chase after him."

"I don't want you to chase after him, he knows his way home." As they came to the small barn door her father said, "Now pull your collar up and here take your walking stick." Scott handed Jane the sturdy walking stick he had

141

made for her years ago. It was always left hanging beside the small barn door.

"Now don't be long, Jane, or I'll have to come looking for you."

"I won't be long, Dad," Jane promised.

Scott Potts watched his daughter to see in which direction she would go, just in case. Watching her walk away, he was reminded of the little girl who could walk for hours in all kinds of weather, alone and unafraid. And who, afterwards would return home to regale the family with all that she had seen on her long walks. For a moment Scott Potts was mentally transported back to the days when his two children were small.

Privately he admitted missing those days. The days when he took them fishing in the nearby brook and their riding in their horse and wagon in the Fourth of July parades and watching them slide down snowy hills on the sleds he had made for them and attending the spelling bees his children competed in. The kaleidoscope of memories spun on and for a moment left him feeling sad that the years of their childhood had flown away so soon. He missed those days. Stubbornly, he rarely admitted he missed those days openly, and never how much he missed them.

Scott went back to finishing up the carpentry work he had started. In the meantime Marjorie's baking was interrupted by the ringing of the telephone.

"Hello."

"Hello, Marjorie?"

"Yes, Ben?"

"Yes, how are you Marjorie?"

"I'm fine, we're all fine, just disappointed you won't be here for Christmas, Ben."

"Ah well, I'm in Philadelphia right now." Benjamin was being cautious, Jane's note only said she was going home. His first thought was their home in Glenwood but he had called there several times with no answer. Finally it dawned on him she must have meant her parents' home.

"Is Jane nearby?"

"No, she is in the barn with her father. Do you want me to go get her?"

"No, that's all right I've had a change in plans and I expect to be at your airport at seven tonight."

"Wonderful, then you'll be with us for Christmas?" Marjorie did nothing to stem her enthusiasm over the news.

"Yes," Ben answered and added. "But I want to surprise Jane."

"That's so nice Ben. I won't tell anyone but I'll pick you up at the airport."

"I don't want to put you out, Marjorie, I'll get a cab. By the way did you get the packages Jane sent up for Christmas?"

"Yes we did, we didn't open the packages but it looks like you two went way overboard by the number of packages.

"It will be so nice to have everyone home for Christmas. Is there something you would like me to bake for you, a special pie, cake, some favorite cookies?"

"No thank you, Marjorie. Whatever you make will be fine."

"All right just don't forget I'll be at the airport at seven tonight, we'll see you then," she reminded him before hanging up.

Marjorie stood thinking after she put down the telephone. She excused the lack of warmth in Benjamin's voice due to whatever he was doing to help his friend. Still, it seemed strange to her that Benjamin apparently didn't have any objections to Jane flying home alone. Marjorie decided she would think more about this when she drove to the airport later on.

Jane cleared the kitchen table and put up her mother's special Christmas treats. According to the Potts Christmas

143

traditions there would be plenty of sampling of the wide variety of baked goods tomorrow night, Christmas Eve.

Marjorie glanced up at the kitchen clock as she was filling the soapstone kitchen sink. "Jane, can I leave you to clean up?"

"Of course Mom, where are you going?"

"I have some errands to run tonight. I'll be back in a couple of hours."

"I'll go with you, Mom."

"No thank you, Jane. I have things to do, I will be back."

As Marjorie was lifting her coat off the coat hook Scott Potts stepped into the kitchen. "Where are you going Margie?"

"I have errands to run."

"Want me to drive you?"

"No I don't, thank you." She smiled at her husband.

"We're expecting more snow, so you be careful."

"I will, besides I'm taking the truck." With a wink Marjorie Potts was out the door.

The small commercial plane landed just as Marjorie Potts stepped into the airport. Benjamin Bradley was one of the first passengers to enter the one-counter terminal. Benjamin spotted Marjorie right away and greeted her with a smile and a hug.

It wasn't long before Benjamin and Marjorie were on the road back to the farm.

"Jane doesn't know I'm coming?" he asked.

"No, you're being here will be a nice surprise for everyone."

"I hope so," he said absentmindedly.

On the slow cautious drive to the airport Marjorie Potts had come to the conclusion that there was some misunderstanding between Jane and Benjamin. Thinking back on the day, Jane never mentioned Benjamin once unless asked specifically about something involving

Benjamin; and at supper Marjorie noted though Jane was animated she never mentioned Benjamin.

Marjorie was concerned. Jane had always been closed mouth. She could not be threatened or forced in any way to speak about something that might be bothering her until she was ready. She wondered if Benjamin in the months they've been married had come to fully understand that aspect of Jane's personality.

Benjamin was talking to Marjorie, but Marjorie's mind was on what Jane might be thinking and the heavy snowfall they were driving through.

"Marjorie?"

"Yes, Benjamin. I'm sorry, Benjamin my mind was somewhere else."

He was smiling. "I could see it was. Last minute things you need to do tomorrow?"
"

"No, not really, I think everything is all set for tomorrow and Christmas Day."I'm just a little tired tonight. But I always am when the holidays come around."

"If you want to pull over I'll drive."

"Thank you, Benjamin, I think I can manage. If not I'll let you know."

Marjorie had been considering whether she should question Ben. "Ben, is there something wrong between you and Jane? I thought it strange that you would let her fly alone when she is seven months along."

"Did Jane say why she came here alone?" Benjamin asked.

"She said you were in Philadelphia helping a friend and fellow surgeon."

"That's all?"

"That's all she said, Benjamin."

"Well that's part of the story. We were in Philadelphia for a reunion of my friends and their wives. Last night there was a dinner party. I got drunk." He hurried on and added, "The first time I got drunk was after my high school

145

graduation. My father found my friend Alex and me dead drunk on a neighbor's lawn. My father was a big man physically and he was a physician. He managed to get both of us back to our house, carry me upstairs, put my friend Alex on the couch and call his father. I was sick for two days and did not take a drink of liquor until last night with the exception of a glass of Champagne on a few rare special occasions."

"Why did you drink last night?"

"For two reasons. One, I was angry with Jane. And angered still when I went up to our room and realized she wasn't there. I didn't see her note until later this morning. I was sick last night and not much better this morning. When I could focus, I read her note. In it she said she was going home. I assumed she meant our home. But every time I called there was no answer. Finally, it dawned on me that she meant her family home. I was not happy she didn't say she was coming here, and that she didn't wait for me to go with her."

"Marjorie, I love Jane, but she can be very stubborn, head strong and at times very annoying."

"What started all of this?"

"That morning, I was the assisting surgeon for my friend Alex. Without telling me, he had Jane called in, as an observer I guess. To make a long story short, Alex is an excellent surgeon, it's just he doesn't exert any discipline in surgery. The kind of conversations that were going on, I would never permit in my operating rooms. On the other hand, Jane didn't seem to mind and contributed to the conversations even after I warned her to stop in a subtle way. She continued. Needless to say the rest of the day and evening were lost for us. She avoided me like a plague. My getting drunk didn't help. Yet, I was surprised she left Philadelphia without me."

"Ben, I love my daughter and all of us think the world of you. The family was disappointed to hear you weren't going to be here for Christmas. But the fact is Jane has always been obstinate, very independent-minded. Somehow she needs to learn as a married woman she is part of a partnership, and differences of opinions need to be discussed and resolved fairly and openly between husband and wife. I imagine it took a lot for you to come here and to tell me about this. I admire that in you and I hope Jane will too.

"Frankly, Benjamin, it won't be easy getting her to change her habits but she can and she must. You two have a baby coming, and you two need to be a solid front for each other and the child. But I believe once Jane adjusts to being married and accepts being part of a vital partnership, you will find her a loyal, loving wife. But I warn you, if you persist in getting drunk she may very well walk out on you for good and frankly I wouldn't blame her.

"And I strongly suggest if there is some behavior of hers you don't like, you need to keep it private between the two of you.

"Now, I will keep this conversation quiet to everyone except my husband. He is very trustworthy and if you like he will talk to Jane. Remember Ben, it takes time to adjust to marriage."

"Thank you Marjorie. I believe that I could trust you and Scott with confidences, and that you both would be fair minded. I would really like to celebrate Christmas and enjoy it with all of you and my Jane. So, I will talk to Jane and hopefully she will be understanding before asking you and Scott to become arbitrators. I want to settle things with my wife and avoid any friction that might reflect on any one else because of unsettled differences between Jane and me."

Josh Potts' little boys were in the kitchen sitting on the table eating cookies from the dish in the center of the table when the door opened and their grandmother and uncle Ben walked in. " Hi grandma!" the boys called out as they

147

scrambled off the table and ran up to Benjamin. "Hi, Uncle Ben!"

"Hi boys, how are the cookies?" He asked with a big knowing smile and a hand on each of the boys' shoulders.

"Good, Uncle Ben, you want some?"

"In a little while, thank you. Where's Aunt Jane?"

"In the parlor playing the piano."

Ben looked surprised. "I didn't know Jane played the piano."

"I taught music in school and piano on the side. I taught Jane to play. She plays very well."

Marjorie turned her attention back to the twins.

The twins eyed their grandmother wondering if she would alert their parents to their "crime." Grandma shook her finger at the boys. "You do remember boys, I personally know Santa Claus and I will see him tomorrow night. Shall I tell him about this?"

"No, grandma," the boys said with genuine sorrow.

"Then you boys had better stay off my table in the future. Good little boys and girls know it's not polite to sit on top of a table. Well behaved, polite children sit on chairs, not tables. Do you understand and will you remember that?"

"Yes, grandma," they replied as they slipped away and quietly joined the rest of the family in the parlor.

"Now that that's settled let's hang up our coats, Benjamin, and join the others."

Ben entered the parlor behind Marjorie and was first spotted by Scott and Josh, Both men stood to shake Ben's hand and wish him a Merry Christmas. Lisa had been the lead singer in singing the carols while Jane played the piano. She too stood up and greeted Ben. Jane stopped playing the piano to see what was happening behind her. Just as she turned around Ben was beside her and kissed her before she could say anything. She smiled at him.

Seeing them together and knowing how much Ben wanted to avoid any semblance of a discord between

148

husband and wife, Marjorie mentally applauded Ben's approach to Jane. She was pleased on two accounts: she had all of her family together for Christmas, and her hopes for Ben and Jane were high. "Isn't anyone going to make coffee for the ones who braved the storm so all of us could be together?" Marjorie asked.

"I'll make it, Marjorie" Lisa volunteered.

After the coffee and cookies for the adults and milk and cookies for the twins, the evening wound down. Josh took his family home with a promise he would be back in the morning to help in the barn.

Ben and Jane said good night to Jane's parents and went upstairs to bed.

The first thing Ben said once they were in bed was, "its freezing."

"It sure is," Jane agreed. You need to wear socks, if your feet are cold the rest of you will be cold; and flannel pajamas are best for winter."

"What are you wearing?" he asked

"Flannel nightgown and heavy woolen socks. I've always kept them here. Better than freezing."

"Isn't there any heat up here?" Ben asked.

"No, this farm has been in my family for over a hundred years. Apparently in all those years no one seemed to think running heat upstairs was necessary, so we all adapted. When it was really, really cold we could bring our bedding downstairs and sleep in front of the fireplace in the parlor."

"Can we do that now?"

"No Ben, there are several blankets and a heavy quilt on this bed and it will be warm enough. You need to put on some socks and a sweater over your pajamas."

Under his breath Benjamin mumbled, "Maybe it's made even colder when my bed mate is cold." Out loud he said, "I'll put on some socks and my sweater, hopefully that will keep me from freezing to death."

Back in bed, Ben suggested, "Let's cuddle, that ought to keep us warm." When Jane didn't respond, Benjamin stretched out his arms and pulled her up to him and began kissing her, on her neck, the front of her face, where ever there was a patch of exposed skin.

Finally, Jane lay nose to nose to him and said. "If you don't stop this I'm going to seduce you!"

Smiling in the darkness Ben responded, "Here, let me help you."

Chapter 17 - Christmas Eve

"Ben, Ben." He heard her voice but did not come fully awake until he felt her attempting to shake him awake.

"What is it, Jane?" he asked in a sleepy voice.

"My father and brother want to know if you'll help them in the barn. They kicked me out, they won't let me help."

Ben slowly sat up and looked at Jane and asked, "What are they doing out there?"

"They are cleaning the barn."

"Why?"

"Because it's Christmas Eve."

Ben yawned. "There has to be more of a reason than its Christmas Eve to clean the barn, but I'll go help after I shower."

"No," She said as she began trying to pull him out of bed. "The story is too long to tell right now and besides you can't take a shower first, you need to get dressed."

"But Jane, I always shower first."

"This is a working farm, Ben. You do your chores first than wash up. After we left last summer Mon washed your dungarees and flannel shirts and hung them up in my closet, and your boots are there too. So get dressed. Oh, and Josh brought over one of his work jackets and a pair of work gloves for you. And hurry up, there is always lots to do on Christmas Eve."

"I'll be down in a few minutes," he called out to her retreating back.

"Mom, Ben will be down in a few minutes. I'm going into the chicken coop. I'll collect and wash the eggs. Do you have anyone who will need eggs today?"

"I don't think so but you never know."

"Are you going to make eggnog today?"

"Yes."

"Okay, then I'll bring in some extra eggs."

"You be careful in the coop, Jane."

"I will, and I'll be in to do up your hair in pin curls when you're ready," Jane said as she rushed outside.

"Good morning Marjorie."

"Good morning Benjamin. Your wife has already headed out to the coop. There's coffee on the stove, help yourself."

"Thank you Marjorie. What are the plans for today?" he asked while pouring himself some coffee.

Without looking up Marjorie continued preparing the turkey for Christmas dinner and said, "We'll be eating a late lunch and a later supper. There is a Christmas Eve service at five tonight that we like to attend. Now, don't feel you have to go Ben, but you're most welcome to join us. Josh has a nice surprise planned for this evening."

She continued on, barely taking a breath. "As soon as we come home Scott and Josh will milk the cows. I will have supper cooking in the kitchen fireplace as always while we're gone. I make stew every Christmas Eve and let it slowly cook. We'll eat as soon as Scott and Josh come in. After supper we go into the parlor and tell Christmas stories and sometimes we read Christmas stories. Sing a few carols and eat Christmas treats. Then Josh and Lisa and the boys go home and have their tree early Christmas morning. We'll have our tree later Christmas morning after the cows are milked and all the animals are fed and watered and Josh and his family are here."

"Sounds nice, I'm glad we're here for Christmas," Ben said. "Do you have the 'T'was The Night Before Christmas' book?"

"Yes, would you like me to get it out for you?"

"If you don't mind I'd like to read it to the twins tonight. My father would always read it to me Christmas Eve. My father had his medical practice in our house. Often there would be interruptions in our evenings and holidays as patients either came to our house or would send for him at all hours. As I look back over the years to my childhood, I

152

remember my father reading to me. He seemed to really enjoy doing that and if he had to put down a book he was reading, he would pick it up later and finish it for me."

Benjamin put his coffee cup down and asked, "Josh left a jacket for me?"

Marjorie pointed to the coat hooks next to the door. "It's the tan one second from the left. He has gloves in one pocket and probably a knit hat in the other pocket."

"Thank you. I'll go see if I can help them," Ben said as he opened the door and went out.

Bending his head against the cold wind Ben hurried along into the barn. It was just after one in the afternoon when the three men came in from the barn. All three sunk into the chairs around the table.

Marjorie's hair was washed and set in pin curls with a kerchief around her head. Jane was washed and smelling fresh, and serving the tired and hungry men. "The coop looks nice Jane, but I thought I told you not to bother."

"Must have forgot, Dad."

"That's convenient, Jane. Consider yourself fortunate it's Christmas Eve and I will not say more about the coop or your forgetfulness."

"She's got away with it again," Josh pitched in.

Jane chuckled. "By the way, how come you guys moved the sleigh?"

"Because tonight we are going to church in high style. We will be traveling by horse and sleigh." Josh said.

"Yeah!!! Who's driving the sleigh?" an excited Jane asked.

"Not you, Jane," her brother piped up.

"Why not, I can drive the buggy and I drove the sleigh once."

"First, it's my surprise for you and Ben. And, second, you drove the sleigh out in the back field and I was with you, little sister, so the answer is no, you are not driving the sleigh!" Josh was emphatic.

Scott stepped in between the siblings' argument. "Josh is right, you do not have enough experience to drive the sleigh, Jane. Josh will be driving you, Ben and Lisa to church while your mother and I will take the twins in the car.

"So that is settled, no more arguments. It is Christmas Eve and I will have peace this special holiday season. You two had better hold your tongues, or you both will answer to me."

"I apologize for my children, Benjamin. For whatever reason, these two have always scrapped every Christmas Eve ever since they were little kids. I don't know what gets into them, but it seems to be inevitable."

Turning to his children, the father added, "It's about time you two started acting like adults so we can all enjoy a peaceful Christmas beginning with this Christmas Eve!"

The peace and quiet that Scott had wanted descended on them as hoped. Marjorie and Jane took their places at the table. In the ensuring silence they all ate slowly with only the sounds of flatware touching dishware.

Josh broke the peace and quiet first. "Dad, isn't it about time we stopped this barn cleaning on Christmas Eve. It seems we all are busy these days, why not do it in the spring or in January during the thaw?"

With sad eyes, Scott looked long at Josh before he spoke. "When the first barn was raised on this land by my ancestors the tradition began, and you know the story, and since that first Christmas Eve here we've never had a barn that burned down nor lost livestock in a fire."

"If you are too busy to help me, Josh, in the future I will hire help so you don't have to come over. But so long as I'm alive, I will keep the tradition going."

Scott Potts got up from the table without another word, took his coat, and walked out the door.

Jane waited until the door closed before lighting into her brother. "How could you say that to Dad? Can't you see he's growing old? He really believes in that story, and if

154

it kills him he will clean the barn by himself every Christmas Eve! After he's gone Josh, you can stop that tradition because he won't be around for you to hurt his feelings..."

"Now Jane, you listen to me...," Josh interrupted.

"No, you let me have my say. If you aren't willing to do the barn cleaning any more, you hire two or three to come and clean Christmas Eve morning. We'll save up some money during the year so we can pay for the hired hands."

"We'll see," Josh answered.

"What do you mean Josh, we'll see?" his sister asked in a surly tone.

Josh lowered his head. "I guess I'm tired of it, is that so hard to understand?"

"No, it's not Josh," Jane spoke with genuine understanding and patience. "But I think we need to make up a little fund and you need to find a couple of farm hands that will be willing to do the cleaning on Christmas Eve."

"I'm not sure Dad will like the idea."

"You heard Dad, he said he would hire help. So Josh, we'll say he can supervise, that way there will be a Potts on the job as prescribed according to tradition. I'll talk to him, Josh, he'll understand. I can't be here to help and you have chores that have to be done on Christmas Eve. Dad must have known there would come a time when we couldn't help," Jane tried to reassure her brother.

Josh rose from his chair, towering above Jane as he always did and said, "Jane, I'm sorry I didn't mean to hurt your feelings or Dad's. You know I love you." Smiling he added, "After all you're my favorite sister".

"Fortunate for me, I'm your only sister," Jane countered with a chuckle.

For a brief moment Josh was his old easy-going self, but Jane suspected all was not well. "Josh, is there something wrong?" Forgetting his mother and brother-in-law were in the room, Josh spoke up to his trusted fishing buddy, Jane. "I don't have a teaching job this winter."

A surprised Jane asked, "Why?"

"I can't say for sure. I guess it's because I had to turn down the fall semester offer. I've been with the College for ten years, and I asked would my not being able to teach that semester hamper my being accepted for the winter/spring semester? The answer I was given was a definite, no, it would not. I need a winter job; I have a family to take care of."

"When did you learn about this?"

"A few days ago. Jane, this has been weighing me down. I still can't believe I won't be teaching during the upcoming semester."

"Have you considered putting your name in the high school? They would be so fortunate to have you teaching, especially the required Civics course."

"You know Josh, I heard someone say, if you need a job let people know. It's the fastest way to get your name out there when you're looking for a job. It seems to me that's sound advice."

"I've been too embarrassed to tell anyone but I have to, I know that." Josh heaved a heavy sigh, He took his sister's hand in his hands. "Thank you, Jane."

"Are you going to sit in on the Church service tonight?"

"I sure am. Jeremy and Johnny are in the Nativity Play."

"Oh, that's going to be interesting!" Jane smiled.

Just then the telephone rang. Josh headed towards the door. "If that's for me just say I'm on my way home."

Marjorie answered the telephone. Smiling she said to the caller, "Yes, we'll be here. See you then."

With both Scott and Josh out of the house, Marjorie stepped over to the kitchen sink and leaned against it as she weighed her thoughts. Benjamin sat quietly at the table looking down at the last few drops of coffee in his cup while Jane silently walked around the family table and quietly sat down facing her mother and asked. "But Mom, why?"

Marjorie then said, "Josh will be teaching at the college this year."

Jane looked puzzled while Benjamin looked up with a questioning expression on his face.

To answer them both she began, "There is a new Dean at the college this year. She roared in with all sorts of, so called modern ideas that most of us simply don't like. In fact many people don't like her. In the short time she has been here, she has alienated a number of people in the College, as well as townspeople. Somehow she was under the impression that being Dean of the college made her queen of this region."

"But back to Josh. First, there were some that took it upon themselves to approach Her Majesty and let her know they wouldn't put up with her arrogance. Second, people did hear about Josh's lost position, and that it was the new Dean that told him he had nothing to worry about even if he couldn't teach the fall semester. The Potts's name means something to folks around here, and things were said and things got resolved. There is a letter from the Dean that will be on our tree tomorrow morning. Santa will deliver it no doubt," She smiled.

Both Benjamin and Jane smiled at the news as Marjorie went on. "Now, he doesn't nor does Lisa know about this. I've been so tempted to tell him but decided that Josh might be better served if he has a sense of what a Christmas miracle might feel like."

Just as Benjamin was about to comment, there was a loud knocking on the door. Benjamin got up from the table and answered the door. Two state troopers were on the porch.

"Mrs. Potts in?" one of them asked.

"Yes, come on in," Benjamin stepped aside to let the troopers in.

The two men stepped over to Marjorie who was smiling at them. "You men have time for some fresh coffee?"

"Thanks, Mrs. Potts, but we have a few more stops to make before night fall."

"Well, let me introduce you to two more members of my family. My daughter, Dr. Jane Bradley, and my son-in-law. Dr. Benjamin Franklin Bradley." Both troopers shook hands with the two Bradleys.

One of the troopers spoke up. "We heard the Potts had a daughter who was a medical doctor."

Jane smiled broadly. "And did you hear I married a medical doctor?"

"Yes," the other trooper said. "And we heard he is a descendant of The Benjamin Franklin."

Jane laughed. "Sounds like you've been talking to my brother."

"He's pretty proud of you and apparently thinks your husband was a good choice on your part!"

"Yup, you've been talking to Josh," Jane exclaimed. "Are you here for the baskets?"

Benjamin raised his eyebrows. Marjorie opened the door to her pantry. "There they are, and they are from all of us."

The troopers picked up the bushel baskets of food and as they moved toward the kitchen door, Marjorie put two bundles of Christmas treats wrapped in wax paper on top of the baskets. "These are cookies for you and the other troopers. Thank you for picking the baskets up, I appreciate it."

"Thank you, Mrs. Potts, we'll see to it they are delivered tonight. A Merry Christmas to you and yours."

"Thank you and Merry Christmas to you and yours too."

After the troopers left, Jane explained to Benjamin, "This family has donated bushel baskets of food since forever, I guess, especially at Christmas. As a matter of fact, most of the farm families around here do the same thing."

"It's time to get ready for church," Jane announced. "Mom, just leave the dishes, I'll do them when we come home. Okay?"

Marjorie looked up at the clock. "Where did the afternoon go?"

"Come on Ben, you need to take your shower and get dressed. Josh will be coming around about four to take us."

"Mom, do you want me to get Dad?"

"No, he will be in soon."

It was a Currier and Ives picture perfect Christmas Eve. Josh drove the Belgian team with an expert hand. Benjamin and Jane sat in the back seat of the open sleigh delighting in the sounds of the sleigh bells ringing as the sleigh glided across the open fields and through the sparkling, lightly falling snow. Too soon, the horse and sleigh ride came to a stop in front of the country church.

Inside the church the smell of balsam boughs and burning bayberry candles scented the air.

Throughout the service, Jane glanced at Benjamin, who held her hand as he had done during the sleigh ride. The expression on his face told Jane he was happy and contented to be there and with her.

After the service, the entire congregation assembled in the basement for refreshments and to socialize. It seemed everyone who attended the service sought out Jane and Benjamin to say a welcoming hello and wish them a very Merry Christmas.

Back at the farm, the chores were done, the meal served and everyone ended up in the parlor. Benjamin asked the boys if they would like him to read the 'T'was The Night before Christmas' story. The twins settled in Benjamin's lap and listened quietly as he read the story. When he finished, the twins thanked him with a kiss and stayed with him until it was time to go.

159

That night Benjamin and Jane cuddled before they began to drift off to sleep. "I love you Jane, Merry Christmas sweetheart."

"Ben, I'm so glad you came. You made this Christmas perfect for me, because, I do love you Ben, big time, and a very Merry Christmas to you too."

Chapter 18 - Happy Birthday

Friday, February 27, 1959 Jane was alone in bed. Benjamin had quietly gotten ready for his day at the hospital early that morning. Sound asleep, Jane had not felt his good-bye kiss.

It was midmorning when she felt the pains. Struggling, she managed to get up and out of bed. Instinctively she knew it was time. On her night stand was the book Dr. Morgan had given her. Inside the book were the telephone numbers Jane believed were important to her penciled in the inside of the front cover. Among those numbers were the numbers to Ben's offices, the hospital ambulance, and the cab company in town. David's office number was printed on the first page of his book. Jane called the cab company first and then David's office.

"Where is Ben?" Morgan asked in an angry tone to no one in particular as he examined Jane in the labor room.

"David, he has surgery this morning, don't bother him," Jane pleaded.

"Sally!" he called to one of the nurses, "Call surgery, find out where Benjamin Bradley is, and have someone tell him his wife is in the labor room."

"NOOO" A sharp pain struck Jane just as she was trying to stop the nurse from calling Ben. Recovering from the pain and breathing hard she said, "David, call his office and let Polly give him the message, please."

Seeing he was upsetting his patient, Morgan relented. "Sally, call Dr. Bradley's office and tell his secretary to let him know his wife is in the labor room."

"Thank you, David; it's not fair to the patient to have his doctor run out on him in surgery."

"You know Jane, you're beginning to think just like him!"

When her labor pains became more frequent, and dilation greater, Morgan decided it was time for Jane to be in the Delivery Room. "It won't be long now Jane, just remember to breathe and push."

Once in the Delivery Room things were moving rapidly. Jane was tiring and tears were welling up in her eyes as she fought to keep from moaning or screaming.

Somewhere in the distance, the sound of a telephone ringing was heard in the Delivery Room. Minutes later the door swung open and Benjamin Franklin Bradley stormed into the Delivery Room.

"Jane." Ben's voice was full and soft as he leaned over his wife and took her hand in his hands. "Honey, I've been calling all over for you, it didn't occur to me to call here first, I'm sorry. They told me in the Labor Room you were here."

"Didn't your secretary tell you Jane was in the Labor Room?" Morgan asked.

"No, I guess she was out to lunch."

"No notes?"

"Didn't see any."

Just then Jane moaned and pushed. "The baby's head is here," Morgan called out. It was in the very next moment that Jane heard a baby cry.

"Jane, we have a little boy." Little Ben's Dad excitedly announced. Ben then kissed Jane and whispered, "Thank you, Sweetheart."

Seconds after little Benjamin let out his first cry, talented, knowledgeable, caring hands proceeded to perform the time- honored practice of preparing the baby for his first day out of the womb and the beginning of his new life.

While Dr. Morgan was taking care of Jane, Benjamin left her side and eased over to where Dr. Ralph Sawyer was finishing up his examination of Ben's little boy.

"How is he?" the father asked.

"He is good and healthy, and I must say he's a good-looking little boy too."

"Thank you Ralph, he looks just like me."

The nurse at Jane's side, hearing Benjamin's remark, smiled broadly. "They are all alike these guys, busting their buttons as soon as they see their babies!"

"Jane, you want to see our baby?" Benjamin asked as he moved carefully over to Jane with the baby in his arms.

"Yes." Jane held out her arms prepared to hold their newborn. Benjamin, however, sat down on the stool beside Jane and held their baby for her to see.

"I think we should put him in his bassinet and take him into the nursery, Dr. Bradley," one of the nurses said, as she gently but firmly took the baby out of his father's arms.

"Do you have a name for him?'

Ben was quick to answer Dr. Sawyer. "His name is Benjamin Franklin Bradley Jr."

"I think it's time for Jane to be tucked into bed too," announced Morgan.

Later Benjamin stood outside the nursery window where several people were assembling. Visiting hours were about to start. Benjamin peered over a couple of visitors as the nursery curtain was pulled back. He quickly picked out his son on the other side of the glass window. When Benjamin spotted him, he again felt the wonder of fatherhood. The light feeling that had begun in his gut now danced in his heart.

It took a while before Benjamin could tear himself away from the nursery window. Finally, he left to make some calls. First he called the florist, next his in-laws; then he stopped in to see Jane in her hospital room. Jane was asleep when he entered her room. He tried to kiss her awake but she slept on.

There would be time, he thought to himself, to tell her all the things that were on his mind and in his heart on this special day, as he went to his office.

Polly Fields was at her desk. His patients were sitting, reading or chatting with other patients. Benjamin could see the relief in their faces as he stepped into his waiting room.

163

He knew then he wouldn't have time to mull over the wonder of the birth of his child any time soon.

Ben looked at Polly, her face was expressionless as he approached her desk. Turning around he faced his patients. "I want to apologize for keeping you waiting. I have a good excuse. About an hour ago, my wife gave birth to our son." Ben proffered his most endearing smile, and just as he was about to turn away a chorus of congratulations surrounded him. Thanking them, he disappeared behind the double doors and soon began seeing his patients.

Hours later Benjamin was able to see the patients he had operated on earlier in the day. Then some time later he was finally able to leave his workday behind and step back onto the maternity floor again. "Hi sweetheart," he greeted Jane as he kissed her and asked,. "Have you held him yet?"

"Yes, he was hungry." She smiled and added, "Like his father he has a good appetite"

Grinning, Benjamin exclaimed, "That's my boy! He wants to eat so he will grow up and be big and tall like me!"

"Honey, sit down, you look tired." Benjamin pulled the padded chair closer to her bed and sighed as he sunk into it.

"I am tired, Jane, but I'm not anxious to go home. You won't be there and I've gotten use to having my wife home with me; besides, I didn't get married to sleep alone as I've told you several times." After saying that, Benjamin got up and planted a long tender kiss on her lips.

Ben sank back down in the chair again as Jane began, "I was thinking, Ben… you know all of this happened; our marriage, our child, all came about because of that one kiss from you in Chicago when we were sitting in my car waiting to go into the terminal."

Benjamin laughed. "You know there were rumors my grandfather Ben was quite the ladies' man in Europe. Maybe besides his name I inherited his charm! If that one kiss sealed you to me and gave me the child I've wanted for

164

so long, than I'm not going to complain. And you had better not either!" He laughed.

"How about a back rub, Dr. Bradley?" A young nurse asked as she stepped into the room.

"I could use one," Benjamin jokingly answered.

"She meant me Benjamin." Jane said. "I'd appreciate it, nurse. Thank you."

"While you have your back rub I'm going to visit with my son."

Benjamin looked into the nursery window for a moment before opening the nursery door in the back and stepping inside the nursery. Wrapping his son in his little blue blanket, Benjamin walked out of the nursery with the baby in his arms.

As he walked along the maternity floor corridor, he stopped as a uniformed State Trooper happened to look out on the corridor as Benjamin came by.

"Dr. Bradley?" Sergeant Liston called out.

Bradley stopped as the trooper stepped out into the corridor. "What have you got there, Doc?"

"My son, he was born today."

The Sergeant looked into the face of the newborn. "He's a cute little guy."

"Thank you, I think he looks like me."

"He does," the sergeant agreed. "Do you have any other children, Doc?"

"No, he's my first one. I've wanted a child ever since I was in my first, ah no, in my third year of medical school. That's where I learned how to make babies." Benjamin laughed. "I was a slow learner," he added to the Sergeant's amusement.

"Well better late than never, so they say!" Liston responded with a smile.

From behind the two men a loud irritated voice called out, "Dr. Bradley!"

"Oh, oh, I'm in trouble," Bradley said in a quiet voice.

"I thought you ran this hospital, Doc?" Liston asked.

165

"My position doesn't mean a thing on this floor! The hounds from hell couldn't get these ladies to bend their rules!"

"Sounds like you know the rules, Doc, don't think you got a leg to stand on,." Liston laughed.

Before Bradley could explain himself to Liston, the Maternity Floor Charge Nurse was breathing down his neck.

"What do you think you're doing, Dr. Bradley, with that baby?"

"Excuse me nurse, this baby is mine. See?" Bradley pulled back the baby's blanket so the nurse could see the baby's name tag. "It says Benjamin Franklin Bradley Junior. I'm Benjamin Franklin Bradley; my son is Junior. And I'm walking him." Bradley beamed.

"Well, Dr. Bradley, Junior has had enough walking tonight. Furthermore, Junior is not going for any more walks with his father while he is in this hospital until his father lets the nurse on duty know he is going to walk the baby and walks him in a bassinet. Now does Junior's Dad understand?

"Now, I will take baby Bradley back to the nursery." Nurse Watson declared as she put out her arms in the mistaken belief she had won the discourse.

Keeping the baby out of the nurse's reach, Benjamin asked, "Where is the bassinet to put him in? My son isn't going anywhere until he is in his bassinet."

The Charge Nurse glared at Bradley and snapped, "I'll go get it!" She then did a smart about-face and headed back to the Nursery.

Turning to the sergeant, Bradley asked, "How much do you want to bet she tells my wife about this and my wife will come down on the nurse's side? Meaning I might have to listen to my wife yell at me!"

Grinning, Liston said, "I've got a free dollar. I'm with you on that one! You, Doc, are going to hear it from the Mrs. Glad it's you and not me!"

It wasn't long before the heavy footsteps of the Charge Nurse were heard fast approaching the rule-breaking father and his witness. "Here is the bassinet, Dr. Bradley."

"Thank you, I'll take him there in a minute."

"You will take him back to the Nursery now!"

"All right, all right, take it easy. I'll bring him back in a minute."

"Okay," she agreed as she turned on her heels again and left the arena of discontent.

Benjamin and Liston watched the nurse hurry down the corridor and step into a patient's room.

Liston looked at Benjamin and asked, "Do you owe me a dollar?"

"That was my wife's room she went into. No, I don't owe you a dollar," Benjamin insisted.

"Well, Doc, take care of yourself, it was nice meeting your son and standing by you."

"Standing by me?"

"If I hadn't been here I would've bet my free dollar that that nurse was mad enough to deck you!!! My advice to you is, pay attention to the rules and stay out of that nurse's way!" Liston's grin widened.

"By the way, what are you doing here?"

"My partner's wife had their second child yesterday. I'm with him."

Early Saturday morning December 17, 1960, Jane rolled over on their bed. "Ben, Ben!" she breathlessly called out.

"What is it, Jane?" a sleepy Benjamin asked.

"It's time, Ben. We have to hurry."

Now wide awake, Ben helped his wife dress, dressed himself and helped Jane into their car. "You need to get Benny!" She called out to him in a panicky voice.

"I know Jane, I won't forget him. I'm going to get him."

Once in the car Benjamin said, "As soon as we get there I'll call Mrs. Mellon. If she can't come to the hospital I'll call Mrs. Stewart. In any case, this time I'll be with you." He promised as he pulled out of the garage, down the driveway and onto the road.

Jane clung to little Ben as Benjamin sped down the country road. "Oh, Ben, I forgot to call David and this one is coming fast."

"Don't worry! As soon as he hears, he'll be there in a flash. Besides, I haven't delivered a baby since my intern days but I think I can remember how. I can always do a c-section, I've done a number of those."

"No C-section Ben!"

"Don't worry, Jane, hopefully you won't need that."

Just then Jane let out a loud moan clutching her stomach ; she bent over, barely avoiding pushing little Benny off her lap.

In record time, Ben pulled in front of the hospital Emergency Room entrance.

"Stay here, Jane, while I get a wheel chair," he said as he dashed out of the car.

In the ER when he called out for a wheel chair, a nurse and an orderly came running. "In my car, my wife and my son." Looking at the receptionist Bradley asked, "Is David Morgan in the house?"

"I don't know, Dr. Bradley. I'll call the main switchboard."

"Is Dr. Morgan in house?" The ER receptionist asked.

Having the answer, she asked the switchboard operator to hold on. "He is not, Dr. Bradley."

"Then ask if he is on call; if so call him, if not call whoever is on call and tell him Jane Bradley is here, and she is in labor." Leaving the receptionist's desk, Bradley looked for and found a phone. He rattled off a phone number to one of the operators and after a short wait a woman answered the call.

168

"Mrs. Mellon, this is Dr. Bradley, I wonder if you could take care of Benny? We are at the hospital, Jane is in labor and we have Ben with us."

"Thank you. I'll see you then."

He went over to the receptionist's desk. "Did they bring out the wheel chair yet?"

"Yes, Dr. Bradley, and they brought your wife up to the Labor Room."

"Where's my son?"

"He's with her."

"I'll head there too, thank you."

By the time Benjamin made it to the Labor Room, Jane was prepped and settled in. Little Ben was outside the Labor Room sitting beside a nurse. When he spotted his father, Benny slipped off his chair and started to crawl towards his father. His father scooped him up into his arms. "Mrs. Mellon is coming here, Benny. She is going to be with you while I am with your mother. You need to be very good, you understand?"

"Why Dabby?" Little Benjamin asked.

"Because Mommy is going to give you a baby brother or a baby sister, so you have to be good while I go help Mommy. You have to stay here with the nurse until Mrs. Mellon comes and be good for Mrs. Mellon. Okay?"

Little Ben shook his head yes.

"Would you let me know when Mrs. Mellon shows up, Nurse?"

"Yes."

"Thank you."

Inside the Labor Room Benjamin positioned himself beside Jane. He asked no one in particular, "Is Dr. Morgan on his way here?"

"I believe he is, Dr. Bradley," one of the nurses replied.

Jane's contractions were coming hard and regularly as tears were welling up in her eyes. "Do you want me to give you an epidural?" Ben asked gently seeing her tears.

169

(I don't think they had epidurals in 1950 – spinals were in then.

"No," she said. Ben covered her clenched hand in his hand to comfort her.

Shortly the labor room door swung open; Dr. Morgan and Dr. Sawyer stepped into the room. Ben was the first person Morgan saw. "Nice to see you here, Ben." Morgan said in an indefinable tone of voice as he stepped in front of Ben and to his patient's side. "Jane, how are you doing?"

She nodded an okay.

"Let me see how close we are," Morgan said as he examined her.

"I think we need to get her into the Delivery Room now." Morgan turned to Benjamin as the moving began. "It was fortunate Sawyer called me right after the hospital called. It's nice we're all together again." And added, "Less than a year later!"

Hearing the sarcasm in David Morgan's voice, Benjamin responded with, "Well you know how it is when you're on a roll..."

Inside the Delivery Room David assured Jane, "It won't be long now, Jane; remember to push and breathe. Do you want some anesthesia?"

"No," she breathed.

Benjamin leaned closer to Jane. Her hand pressed harder into his hand. He spoke to her in a low soothing voice and stroked her hair as she pushed, breathed and hoped for the best.

Just when Jane seemed to be too tired to do more, she gave one last gallant push and was rewarded with the lusty cries of their second son.

Benjamin bent over and kissed her and said once again, "Thank you, sweetheart." Then Ben walked over to Dr. Sawyer and watched as Sawyer prepared Baby Bradley for his new life.

"Do you have a name for this little guy?" asked Dr. Sawyer.

170

"Yes, his name is Scott Allen Bradley," answered the proud Dr. Benjamin Bradley.

Hearing the name for the new baby Jane called to Ben. "Ben, I thought you were going to name him Allen Scott Bradley."

"I decided Scott Allen Bradley sounded better. So when Scott is old enough to get into mischief and you start yelling at him using all three of his names, at least hearing you yelling his names won't be grating if you begin with Scott. My name sounds good and that's why it isn't grating when you're yelling at me!" he grinned.

"Benjamin Franklin Bradley, how dare you say that in front of other people?"

Laughing he answered, "because it's true."

Looking over his shoulder, Benjamin asked the grinning Sawyer, "Are you all done Ralph?"

"Yes, did you want to hold him now?"

"Yes, I want to hold my little Scott Allen."

As Ben took his son from Dr. Sawyer, Sawyer noted, "This one looks just like you too, Ben."

"Fortunate little guy!" Benjamin smiled.

Chapter 19 - Out of the Past

For years Benjamin had two projects near and dear to his medical heart. It took years to negotiate successfully with the Medical School in Overlook, Overlook Memorial Hospital and the State to institute accredited Intern and Resident programs in Switzer Hospital. His first project completed and running smoothly, the idea of working towards his second project, the development of a medical research facility on Switzer's grounds, now seemed just right.

By deciding it was time to proceed on that project Benjamin discovered he had opened the floodgate to an army of vendors and other enterprising interests all wanting his attention, even though he made it clear to all interested parties it would be years before there would be a go-ahead on the project. At the time it was just an exploratory project to investigate costs to create such a facility, and learn of the latest test equipment and medical products used for research.

"Dr. Bradley, Dr. Jane Bradley." Her page reached her in the office Dr. Sawyer used in the Switzer Hospital doctors' offices once a week when he was instructing Residents and seeing some patients including the Bradley boys.

Elizabeth, Dr. Sawyer's part-time receptionist and full-time wife called out to her, "Jane, why don't you use this phone?" she said, gesturing towards the phone on her desk.

"Thank you," Jane said as she picked up the telephone. After listening to the caller Jane responded, "I'll be right there."

"Elizabeth, I have to go to the ER, can I leave my boys here? I'll come back for them when I finish up in the ER?"

"Of course, they will be fine. I'm leaving at noon but Barbara will be here by the time I have to leave."

"Thank you, Elizabeth."

"Benjamin, Scott, Mommy has to go to the ER. I want you two to stay here until I come for you. Do you understand?"

"Yes," they said as they nodded their heads.

"All right then, you can play with the toys that are here, so be good."

Jane flew out of the pediatrician's office confident the boys would be fine.

About two hours later, the door to the Hospital Administrator's Conference room swung wide open. Jane's eyes quickly scanned one side of the room to her right. At the far end on that side of the Conference room she saw two small souls quietly sitting at one of the conference tables busy coloring in coloring books. Despite the relief at seeing her children safe and sound, Jane called to her sons. "Benjamin Franklin Bradley, Scott Allen Bradley, come here!" Jane's loud angry voice reached every corner of the conference room and spread throughout the whole room. On the opposite side of the room were four adult figures sitting at one of the conference tables on the far left. If Jane saw the adults, they did not register in her thinking. Her entire focus was on the two little boys.

Hearing the anger in their Mother's voice, the little Bradley boys got up from their chairs and walked with hesitant steps towards her. Across the room the four men turned around and watched the sad parade with deep pity in their hearts for the little guys.

The tallest and the biggest of the men quietly broke away from the group and slowly moved towards the angry mother. Finally the repentant boys stood before their mother in absolute silence.

"All right Benjamin. You are the oldest. What did I tell you two to do?"

"Stay here," the little voice stated.

"Until when?" Jane prompted.

"'Til you come," Little Benjamin answered.

173

"Until I came," Jane corrected.

"Right." Little Scott answered.

"Okay boys, how did you get up here?"

Before Little Benjamin answered ,he glanced sideways and upwards and hope rose in his heart. He saw his father standing behind his mother. Benjamin pointed upward and said solemnly, "Dabby do bit!"

"What did Daddy do, Benjamin?"

"Dabby brought us here."

"Why?" their mother asked.

From behind her a strong male voice answered. "Because they were wandering around in the hallways."

Jane swung around. "Why were they wandering around in the hallways?"

"They said Mommy said it was okay."

That answer only annoyed her all the more. Pointing to where the boys had sat she ordered, "You boys go down to the table and pick up whatever you were playing with and put it back where you found it." With that the two boys took off running like a couple of escaping convicts, to comply with those orders.

"Why didn't you page me if they were on the loose? Seems everybody else manages to page me with no trouble."

Just then they heard a familiar page: "Dr. Bradley, Dr. Jane Bradley."

"Like that," she said as she swung around and took angry steps towards the telephone on the desk behind them. "Jane Bradley here," she answered in a calmer tone.

"Yes, thank you, operator."

"Mrs. Mellon, you are a godsend. My sons are up here on the seventh floor in the conference room. Let me check. Ben, is there a door open to the back seat of your car?"

"Yes."

"Yes, Mrs. Mellon, the boys' car chairs are in the back seat of their Dad's car. Do you want me to bring the boys

174

down to you? That will be fine, thank you Mrs. Mellon, we'll expect you here then."

"Did you put those things away, boys?" Their mother asked as she looked their way.

"Yes," they answered together.

"Come here."

The boys stood once again in front of their mother. She began, "Since everyone in this hospital thinks I flipped my wig thanks to you two, I have a mind to spank all three of you Bradley boys when I get home tonight and send all three of you to bed without dinner! I suggest you two stay out of trouble for the rest of the day. Do you understand?"

"Yes," a small sad voice responded. Little Ben looked up at his mother and asked, "You going to spank Dabby too?"

"I might," his mother answered.

All of a sudden Little Ben started crying as he ran over to his father with his arms up in the air. "I sorry Dabby."

Benjamin scooped up his son and held him tightly. Little Scott followed his brother and held up his arms and Benjamin scooped him up and held him tightly too.

Jane sighed, and slowly ambled away from the three Bradleys and headed towards one of the windows that looked down on the parking lot and beyond.

She walked past the three men who had lost Benjamin's attention the moment Jane entered the conference room. One of the three men appeared to be studying Jane as she looked out the window.

Minutes later, Jane turned around and walked back towards Benjamin and the boys. It wasn't long before Mrs. Mellon walked into the Conference Room. "Hi guys!" she greeted the boys. They responded warmly to her with bright smiles and arms out. Benjamin kissed the top of both boys' heads before letting them go to Mrs. Mellon.

"Do you have their car chairs, Mrs. Mellon?"

175

"Yes. Oh and my husband is going to put in those raised vegetable beds for you today. That ought to keep the boys busy."

"Good," she smiled. "All right Benny, Scotty you be good boys and have fun in the garden." Jane started to bend down to kiss the boys but they turned quickly and went off with Mrs. Mellon.

Sighing, Jane pulled out a chair from under the conference table and sank in it as she watched her children skip happily down the corridor while holding Mrs. Mellon's hands. Jane created a pyramid with her forearms and rested her chin on her thumbs as tears began to well up in her eyes. Benjamin quietly pulled out the empty chair beside her and sat down in it with his handkerchief in hand. "Here," he said as he handed her his handkerchief.

Jane dabbed at her eyes as she spoke in a soft shaken voice. "Oh Ben, I thought I had lost them. I opened every closed door, I ran up every stair well between floors. All I could think was some stranger had my children. And, for a moment I thought about killing who ever took my children. I've never thought about killing anyone in my life! It is a very ugly feeling to even consider that awful deed. But I was so afraid for them!" Jane was shaking as she spoke. Ben put his arms around her and held her tight and as close to him as possible.

"Yet, they didn't even look at me as they left. That broke my heart." She spoke in a quivering voice as her tears flowed freely down her cheeks.

Quietly Benjamin said, "Maybe, Jane, you should show them your tears more often than your anger. They would understand you, don't want them hurt, and tears would reassure them that you do love them. They are so young that we can't expect them to think like adults or understand like adults."

Jane nodded she understood. "I just want them to realize there are dangers. They are so innocent, they trust everyone."

"I know, we'll just have to carefully instill in their little minds not everyone is good. And Jane," he added with strong conviction, "they love you, you know that." Benjamin lifted her and himself out of their chairs as he hugged her. Jane encircled him with her arms. And as always Ben's calming nature soon worked its curative magic on Jane. Now she was able to relay an incident that had occurred as she was searching for the boys.

"While I was looking for the boys, I ended up opening doors along the corridors."

"And you opened a door you shouldn't have. Right?"

"Right I opened one door and this man yelled this is a men's room!. He was standing at an open stall. I yelled back I'm looking for two little boys. 'They aren't here,' he said and then he rudely yelled, 'Get out!'"

I yelled again, "I'm a doctor and you don't have anything I haven't seen before and better!"

Ben burst out laughing. "That wasn't nice, you shouldn't have said that."

"Honestly I didn't care what I said, besides I couldn't see any part of him, he was in the last stall. If he thinks about it, he will know I couldn't see any part of him. Besides I had more to worry about than protocol in the men's room. I hope he wasn't someone that knows you."

"I hope he wasn't a prospective donor to this hospital or the research center. If he is I'm going to have to hide you!" he joked.

Later that afternoon Jane's day as a full fledged pediatrician was coming to an end when her receptionist called her into her office. "Dr. Bradley, there is a gentleman here to see you."

Jane answered, "Send him into my office will you? I am going over some charts. Thank you Barbara."

Jane's office door was open. "Jane."

Jane Bradley looked up from the chart in her hand and into the face of Matt Hunter. She was very surprised and smiled broadly as she stood up and exclaimed, "Matt!"

177

Matt leaned across her desk and kissed her lightly on her lips. She gestured towards the chair in front of her desk. "Have a seat." She was still smiling as she watched him settle in the chair.

"I'm finding it hard to believe that you're here," she said.

"It was a very pleasant surprise for me to see you, Jane. Over the years I had wondered if I would ever see you again, and then when I decided I would never see you again, here we are," he smiled.

Jane slipped back into her chair still finding it hard to believe Matt, her first love, was sitting in her office.

"You know your father wouldn't say where I could find you. The last time I called your parents they told me you were married. The hospital in Chicago wasn't any help either, they wouldn't tell me where you were doing your residency. So, here we are years later. I had to stop and see you, Jane. I'm not sure if your husband knows who I am."

"I don't know if he remembers your name. I did tell him about you."

"He seems like a nice guy."

"He is very nice and I love him dearly."

"Those two boys yours and his?"

"Yes, they are, why do you ask?"

"There was a time I dreamed about you and me having children. I loved you very much, Jane. When your father didn't call me back, I thought you probably told him not to. It took me months to get up the nerve to call him back and that's when he told me you were married."

"I married a couple of years later. I have a little boy."

Just then Barbara stepped into Jane's open office door. "Come in, Barbara."

"I'm done for the day, Dr. Bradley, just wanted you to know I'm leaving."

"Thank you,. Barbara; anything I need to know now?"

"Just your first appointment is at 8:20 tomorrow morning."

"I'm not on call tonight am I?"

"No, it's Dr. Sawyer's turn."

"Oh good, he had an easy day today." Jane smiled. "Thank you, Barbara, I'll see you tomorrow."

Jane now turned her attention back to Hunter. "Are you here about the proposed Research Facility?"

"Yes, I am. Jane, I can't begin to explain my surprise when I saw you. You looked so sad standing at the window, I wanted to put my arms around you and comfort you."

Jane looked long at Matt Hunter. She realized he was more handsome than she remembered. And for a moment she almost raised her arms to brush her hair with her hands just in case it was a bit mussed up. Jane resisted that temptation in time.

She did, however, remember his charm and knew it was important to keep their conversation from slipping into past remembrances. So, Jane stated bluntly but quietly,. "I'm not on the project's board. I wouldn't even consider trying to influence Ben on this matter. Like everyone else, I trust Ben's judgment. I'm afraid I can't be of any help to you, Matt."

"Besides, I have enough to do being a wife, a mother and a doctor and in that order. I don't volunteer for anything either." She smiled. "Matt, it has been very nice seeing again. You look well and I'm glad of that." She added with sincerity, "I wish you well always."

Hunter smiled and nodded a thank you. The charm he had loved about Jane was still with her, he noted.

"To tell you the truth Matt, it's been a very long day, I am very tired and I have things I have to do when I get home."

"Like spank the three Bradley boys?" Matt asked with a grin.

Laughing, Jane responded, "Frankly, my bark is worse than my bite and furthermore I don't have the energy to

179

spank those rascals. And worse, the three of them probably know that!"

"Jane, I didn't come here to ask your help in my business. I wanted to see you. I can hardly believe you are actually here with me."

"Matt, I do wish you and yours well. It's just that..."

He interrupted her. "Jane, I was hoping you would have coffee with me."

"I can't, Matt. I am married and you are married. We don't need any scandal.

"Besides, I am happy in my marriage, and I hope you are in yours. I won't do anything that might cause a stir in my marriage.

"Ben believes that there are things in life that are meant to be. He believes we were meant to be. He is always right in these matters. I guess you and I were not meant to be together. Thank you for the invitation but I think I'll go home." Jane smiled as she stood up and was about to usher Matt out when Benjamin suddenly stepped into Jane's office blocking Matt's way out.

"Hunter." With a nod Benjamin acknowledged Jane's first love. Hunter in turn acknowledged Benjamin with a nod. "Am I interrupting?" Benjamin asked.

"No, I was just leaving," Hunter said.

Benjamin stepped aside and Hunter passed by him without another word. Ben then turned to Jane and asked. "Are you on call tonight?"

"No," she answered.

"Good, we'll leave your wagon here and you can go home with me."

"I can." Jane was a little wary about driving home with Ben but decided if he was going to talk about Matt she preferred the discussion take place in the car rather than with the children in ear shot.

Once in the car, Jane sighed a tired sigh while Benjamin drove in silence. It wasn't long before Jane realized they weren't heading home. She sat quietly wondering where they were going.

Finally, Jane recognized the area. It was the Ridge. Now, she knew the Ridge could be approached by another route, a route she was not familiar with.

Ben pulled up in front of the locked gate. Without a word he reached across Jane and took the key from the glove box. After unlocking the gate he drove through, then stopped and stepped out of the car to close and lock the gate, as usual, before driving across the field and up to the top of the Ridge.

Once parked on the Ridge, Benjamin got out of the car and went over to the passenger side of the car and opened the door for his wife.

Even as Jane got out Ben's car, Benjamin remained silent. Jane moved a few feet away from the car, making a pretense of interest in the nearby early spring growth of wild flowers and budding wild bushes.

Ben watched her for a few minutes before walking over to her. Her head was still bowed. "I prize loyalty, Jane," he stated as he stood before her, with her head now up and looking him straight in the eyes. "What did he want?" he asked.

"He just wanted to say hello," Jane answered.

"Is that all?"

"Yes, I told him that I have no influence in the research center project."

"Did he ask for your help in influencing the project?"

"No, he didn't, it was what I thought he wanted."

"It didn't occur to you that he might have wanted time with you?"

"Ben, he asked me if I would have coffee with him and I said no. He is married and I am married, and I don't want any complications. I made that clear to him."

"He still in love with you?"

"He didn't say he was. I don't think he is. What difference does it make? I don't love him."

The way Benjamin was looking at Jane it was as though he was wondering if all the cards were on the table or did someone have a card up their sleeve. He was beginning to feel guilty questioning Jane's loyalty to him. Jane had never given him reason to be jealous, he just wanted to be sure.

"He's younger than I am," Benjamin stated as a matter of fact, not necessarily implying anything specific. Jane did not respond to his statement. "I guess one could say he's good looking. Like a cowboy in the movies or something." Jane looked puzzled. "Well?"

"Well, what Ben?" Jane asked.

"I need to know."

"Need to know what, Ben?" Jane asked.

"That you are loyal to me."

Jane's annoyance with Ben was quickly turning to anger. "Tell me when I have not been loyal to you, Ben!"

Ben did not respond. His silence caused Jane to become angrier.

She exploded. "Ben, I've had enough of this stupid conversation. Now, you can give me the keys to the car and I'll drive us home, or if you rather I didn't go home I will walk to the nearest hotel and stay there. Either way I don't care!"

Still Ben said nothing. It was as though he was in a state of shock. He saw Jane round the car, open the passenger's side door and reached in and grabbed her handbag. Turning around she began to walk off the top of the Ridge. Yet he did not react right away.

Ben snapped out of his stupor-like state as he saw her head down the path to the base of the Ridge. "Jane!" he called after her.

Hearing Ben call to her made Jane step up her pace. She reached the base of the Ridge in extraordinary fast time. When she reached the gate she had no way of unlocking it, and knew she was unable to climb over the barbed wire fence. She was effectively trapped.

It wasn't long before Benjamin was at the gate in his car. He got out of the car with the key to the gate in hand. "Get in the car Jane! I've had enough of all this!"

Jane stood her ground. "No."

Her response surprised him. "What do you mean, no?"

"I've had enough, I'm leaving you."

"Leaving me? Why, so you can be with Hunter?"

"No, because I've had enough of you!"

"That's too bad Jane, because I will not give you a divorce, and I will not give up my children. Now get in the damn car so we can go home!"

"No!" she exclaimed.

"What?"

When it appeared Jane was not moved by Benjamin's growing anger, he took a menacing step towards her.

Suddenly without warning Jane asked in a calm voice, "What did she die of?"

Taken aback by the question Benjamin asked, "Who?"

"Luanne," she answered.

"Cancer. Why?" He asked, puzzled.

In a calm quiet voice she answered, "I wondered if she had died of a heart attack or perhaps a broken heart." Benjamin, she knew, was listening to her every word and wondering where this discussion was going. She went on. "Sometimes I think you miss the good old days when you had the perfect wife beside you. The beautiful, sophisticated Luanne instead of the plain Jane you've been stuck with these past five years."

Benjamin was worried. He wondered if seeing her former lover had triggered some hidden resentment towards him.

Trying to understand her thinking, he ventured, "I've told you Jane, she's dead and she does not stand between us."

"She is dead Benjamin, but I feel like I am walking in her shadow and I am awkward and stumbling compared to her."

"As to the good old days, those are the days that I, no, you and I, are living. I don't miss her but I do miss you. Now please get into the car and let's go home."

Jane hesitated at first then slowly stepped over to the door Benjamin held open for her and got into the car. Inside the car silent tears flowed down her face. Behind the wheel of his car Benjamin looked at Jane. Seeing her tears, he moved over to her. Heaving a heavy sigh Benjamin wrapped his arms around Jane and pressed her close to his heart. "You are not walking in her shadow. You are beautiful in ways she could never be. You have a lasting inner beauty. I swear that is the truth and I love you Jane more than I can begin to tell you."

Jane lifted her head up. "But I thought."

"I don't know what you thought but I do know you have made me happier than I have ever been in my adult life. It is time to forget this nonsense of shadows. There are no shadows, Jane. No one stands between you and me. I do not regret marrying you, Jane. It's just I do not want anyone to come between you and me, ever."

Chapter 20 - A Winter's Brew

"Dr. Benjamin Bradley, Dr. Benjamin Bradley." The page didn't reach the operating room where Dr. Benjamin was operating on an elderly patient.

A young student nurse rushed into the operating room. "Dr. Bradley, there is an emergency call from the State Police for you."

Benjamin looked away from his patient for a quick moment. "I can't leave my patient. Ask the caller to give you a name and phone number and I'll call back."

"Okay Doctor," she said as she rushed out of the room.

Moments later she was back again. "Dr. Bradley, they want to know how long you'll be."

Heaving an annoyed sigh, Bradley answered, "Tell them in a few minutes."

"Okay." Again, the young nurse rushed out.

A couple of minutes went by and the assisting surgeon said, "I'm waiting for another breaking news report."

"Let's hope that was the last of the news flashes," Bradley said. "Will you close for me, Fred?"

Unfortunately for Dr. Bradley, his surgical staff and everyone on duty at the Switzer and Overlook Hospitals that Wednesday February 5, 1964, the rush of news flashes was just beginning.

Dr. Bradley left surgery and was heading to his office on the seventh floor that morning when his page again resonated along the corridors.

"I'll pick it up in my office," he thought to himself as he entered the elevator.

Marsha was on the telephone when he walked into his Hospital Administrator's Office. "Just a minute," she said to the caller. "He's just coming in."

Benjamin nodded in Marsha's direction as he shuffled past her desk and into his office, then sank down into his chair. Of late, Benjamin had been toying with the idea of retiring from either his surgical practice or resigning his position as Hospital Administrator.

What he really wanted to do was to move to Florida, buy a house boat and a small fishing boat, and become a fishing guide to the tourists. That was his dream, but Benjamin didn't think he could earn enough money to support Jane, their two sons and the new baby they were expecting in March, on a fishing guide's earnings.

Outside cold swirls of snow were moving across the snowed-in fields and parking lots. With a vision of warm sands, palm trees swaying in a light breeze and a sparkling blue ocean beneath a bright sun still in his mind's eye, and with a longing sigh Benjamin picked up the telephone receiver on his desk and answered, "Dr. Bradley."

"Dr. Bradley, this is Major Taylor at the G troop barracks. We have two commercial planes down. Several injured that need medical help right away. We are transporting to your hospital and to Overlook. Switzer is closer and so we are bringing the more serious to your hospital."

"All right, we'll do our best," Benjamin responded.

"Thank you, your secretary has all the information she needs to reach me."

"Good," Ben answered.

Benjamin's next call was to Marsha. "Marsha, page all the department heads and physicians in this hospital; we need to have an emergency meeting in the Conference Room, right away. Thank you."

Last he called home, told Jane what had happened and told her not to expect him home for dinner, and that he had no idea when he would be home. When Jane asked if she could be of help, he said he didn't think so at present. But he did say that a storm was expected to move into their area the next day. He suggested she get groceries in anticipation of the storm, before the day was over.

All available medical personnel were called in. Nurses, orderlies, medical and x-ray technicians were asked to stay

186

on, interns and residents were sent into the ER to set up and man a triage. The cafeteria and the coffee shop personnel were told to stay open, and to be sure to keep the coffee coming and keep orange juice ready for the surgical staff.

The practice sessions requested by Civil Defense that Switzer performed under Bradley's directions had paid off in this emergency. As Thursday February 6 was coming to a close, Switzer had returned to near normal. Most of the extra help needed for this emergency were able to go home and catch up on some sleep. The last to go home were the department heads and eventually the Hospital Administrator.

But before anyone left, Dr. Bradley spoke to all of the hospital personnel over the PA system, thanking them for their dedication and fine performances. He credited the efforts of all of the hospital personnel for the survival of all the patients who had been transported to Switzer from the crash site.

Before Benjamin could leave the hospital he had paper work to take care of for the Board, and instructions to write for Polly and Marsha. The first thing he asked Polly to do was to cancel all of his appointments for Friday. While he was writing instructions to Marsha, Amy Walters stepped into his office.

"I thought I saw you come in here, Ben. I wanted to tell you how impressed I was with your performance in surgery. You have incredible stamina..."

"For a man my age?" he interrupted, and asked with a grin as he reluctantly put down his pen and gave Amy his full attention as she sat down in the chair across the desk from him.

"You're not old, Ben."

Benjamin smiled broadly "I feel like I'm a hundred years old right now. It's been a long two days."

"It sure has," she replied.

"And as always Amy, your performance in surgery was admirable, I really appreciated your coming in to help."

"I've always said any time you need me, I'm here for you.

"You know Ben, Stan and I were saying the other day we see so little of you since you married."

"Well, I have a wife that wants my attention ninety percent of my time, my two little boys think I'm Superman and can give them one hundred percent of my time, so we have little time for anyone else. My family keeps me busy. I'm not complaining just explaining.

"Jane and I were saying, not long ago, we need to get out a little more, visit friends," Ben nodded in Amy's direction as a reminder of his friendship with Amy and her husband.

"I think those plans are on hold for a while longer, we're expecting another baby next month."

"So I heard. How old are your children now?

"Benjamin will be five the 27 of this month. Scotty turned four December 17."

"I heard Jane completed her residency about a year ago?"

"Yes, she did."

"What about you, Ben?"

Amy stood up and walked suggestively, slowly around Ben's desk until she was beside him.

Benjamin turned in his chair just as Amy placed her hands on the arms of his chair and leaned down and forward.

"It sounds like there isn't anything special for you."

He didn't understand what she meant and stared at her trying to find meaning in her words. During this confusion Amy stepped in closer to Benjamin and planted a long, passionate kiss on his lips before telling him., "I can make life more exciting for you, Ben, and the best part is Stan would understand."

Benjamin maneuvered his way out of his chair so as not to touch Amy in any way, now that he understood Amy's meaning. "Amy, let me explain something to you. First, let me say you flattered me, but do you know what my wife would do if I wandered onto another pasture?" When Amy didn't answer Benjamin continued. "She would pack up the kids' things and her things, put the boys in her car and leave and never let me know where she and our children were. A toss in the hay isn't worth the loss of my wife and children.

"Amy, you are an exceptional surgical nurse, you are also the wife of a friend of mine, so I'm going to pretend this discussion never took place. I suggest you forget all of this too.

"If you'll excuse me Amy I need to finish this memo. I want to go home."

"You know, Ben, I'm not used to being snubbed..."

Bradley interrupted her, "I said I was flattered Amy, and I meant it. I did not snub you, I wouldn't do that, but the fact is I am very happy with Jane, I am very grateful she is my wife, I'm not looking around."

Amy stepped back. "Ben, I could make you incredibly happy and probably far better than Jane can, or does!" With that Amy turned around and left.

Ben was stunned. He wasn't sure if Amy was angry with him, or Jane. In any case he wasn't worried, he thought he knew Amy.

It was almost three in the morning, Friday, February 7 when Benjamin pulled into his garage and stepped into the warmth of his home. On the kitchen counter he spotted something under the cover of a clean cloth. He peeked under the cover and smiled. Jane had made one of Ben's favorite desserts, pineapple upside down cake. In the refrigerator there were leftovers, fried chicken, tuna casserole and meat loaf. As he looked at the food in the refrigerator, he thought again of what he said to Amy. He was glad he had married Jane. He had no regrets.

He left the kitchen and walked toward the bedroom area. Benjamin stopped at his boys' bedroom and quietly pushed wide open the slightly ajar door. Stepping into the

189

room he could see by the hallway light Jane always left on, for their sleeping children. He smiled as he looked at them. Seeing all was well with them, he left their room and crossed the hallway and into his and Jane's bedroom.

Jane always left a light in their bathroom on, and the bathroom door slightly ajar so there would be a streak of light in their bedroom. In that bit of light he saw she was sleeping peacefully. Seeing her asleep, he wanted nothing more than to get into bed and snuggle up to her.

Benjamin slid in beside her and gently took her into his arms.

"Ben?" he heard her ask in a soft sleepy voice.

"Were you expecting someone else?" He smiled in the semi-darkness.

Unexpectedly, Jane's arms suddenly came up, rounded the sides of his chest and held Ben gently while she moved up to him and buried her face into the side of his face. "I'm glad you're home, I missed you."

Jane held Ben, kissing him with a sweetness that touched the depth of his soul. They lay in each other's arms so close that Ben could feel the baby in Jane's belly move against his stomach, in what Ben could imagine were happy leaps from his yet-to-be-born youngest child.

It was a long while before Benjamin and Jane finally fell asleep settled in each other's arms.

One thing was certain, Ben would never forget that very private time between husband and wife that early morning. And in the future, his memory of that time would comfort and sustain him...

At the reasonable hour of seven that Friday morning, Jane quietly slipped out of their bed and hurriedly threw on her bathrobe and slippers in hopes of beating her children to the kitchen. Her thoughts were set on enjoying a quiet moment or two with a fresh brewed cup of coffee before her day began.

Jane sat at the table with coffee cup in hand patiently waiting for the coffee pot on the stove to begin percolating.

She savored these quiet moments in the morning. They helped her to begin her day on the bright side of things. Glancing out of the kitchen windows she was glad her office in Switzer, and Dr. Sawyer's office in Overlook were closed for the day. The storm had begun. She hoped there would be no emergencies she would have to respond to today.

Jane was drinking her second cup of coffee when she glanced up at the kitchen clock, a frown creased her face. The boys had not come into the kitchen yet. They usually showed up after she had a couple sips of her first cup of coffee. Jane left her place at the table to see why the boys were late to the breakfast table.

She looked into their room, their beds were empty. Looking across at hers and Ben's room the door was wide open. She had left it ajar.

Jane quickly stepped into the room. The boys were just climbing into the bed from her side of the bed giggling as they went. She rushed over to them as they reached the top of their Mount Everest. She whispered as she grabbed the first child and started what became a little tug of war. Scotty clutched the sheets and hung on as his little legs moved up and down as his mother tried to pull him off the bed. In the meantime Little Benjamin had reached his destination and was about to slam into his father's chest.

Seeing where her older son was, Jane let go of Scotty and tried to reach little Benjamin before impact. But her cry of "Stop!" did not deter her older son, however. Ben who had been awakened earlier by the boys' loud whispers and only pretended to be asleep, had only to put his hand out and little Benjamin stopped his approach.

"Oh Ben, I thought you were asleep."

"I was until I heard these little connivers planning their assault on their old man." He laughed as he sat up. "I might as well get up, what's for breakfast?"

191

Outside the snow storm raged on. Inside the Bradley family spent a cozy, quiet day in the parlor.

Ben read aloud, the boys played with their farm set, while Jane finished knitting the set of matching sweater, hat and booties she had begun making for the new baby a few months before.

It was the perfect family day, one to remember.

"Did Sawyer get off today?" Benjamin asked as the four sat down for the family dinner hour.

"No, he changed their flight so he and Elizabeth and their children could leave early yesterday morning ahead of this storm."

"Where did they fly out of?"

"New York City. They drove there the day before."

"So, you are covering for him the rest of this week and all next week too?"

"Yes."

"Isn't that's a little too much for you, Jane?"

"It would be if he hadn't closed his office for vacation and fortunately there hasn't been any emergency to handle. So, it's been easy duty," she smiled.

"Oh, that reminds me, I called your office Tuesday and told Polly that I was covering for Ralph should any calls for him or me come in, to please give them my office number and my home number. You know how people see Bradley or hear Bradley they immediately call your office."

"Funny, she didn't tell me you called."

"Well she might have been busy. Besides, it isn't something you needed to know, it was just a request to redirect phone calls for me should that be necessary."

After dinner that evening Ben took charge of bathing the boys and getting them ready for bed. Jane picked up the kitchen before retiring to the parlor where Ben joined her. "Are they all tucked in?"

"They are bathed and in their pajamas, read to, prayed with and tucked in. Anything else and they would have to tuck me into bed."

"Benjamin, are you ready to go to bed?"

"Yes, I am."

Once in bed Jane remembered something. "I'll be right back; I almost forgot."

Jane slipped out of bed turned on the lamp on her dresser then reached down and pulled out the bottom drawer. She lifted out something wrapped in white tissue and placed it on top of her dresser alongside the baby sweater, booties and hat set she had finished knitting that day.

Turning off the light she made her way back to the bed and into it. Turning on his side facing Jane, Benjamin asked, "What did you forget?"

"The blanket I had knitted first to go with the hat, sweater and booties for the baby."

"So, why did you take them out now, are you having labor pains?" Ben sounded worried.

"No, I just wanted all the pieces to the set together so when it's time to bring the baby home you'll find everything in one place so you can bring them to me in the hospital, and I can put them on the baby before we come home."

"Oh, okay," Ben smiled in the darkness.

As the night time hours grew, the storm's fury was beginning to lessen. Sometime around one the next morning the telephone rang, splitting apart the peace and quiet in the Bradleys' bedroom.

"Dr. Bradley," Benjamin answered in his alert tone of voice.

After listening to the caller he said, "Just a minute; you want to talk to Dr. Jane Bradley."

"Jane, Jane," Ben called to her.

"What is it?" she asked in a sleepy voice.

"Telephone," he said as he stretched out his arm with the telephone handset in her general direction.

"Thanks," she said with little enthusiasm as she took the telephone piece from his hand. And into the phone she said, "Dr. Jane Bradley."

193

Jane did not recognize the voice or the name on the telephone. She did however recognize the symptoms of a serious condition. "And the baby is how old?"

After hearing the age of the baby Jane said, "You need to get the baby to the hospital. Which hospital are you closest to?"

"Overlook," was the reply.

"All right, I'll meet you there, Mrs. Carter."

Chapter 21 - The Trial

It was an unusual trial. The Court Room was packed with the curious. And like the curious spectators, none of the twelve members of the jury were prepared for the shocking testimony that would be revealed during this trial.

"Your name and occupation?" Prosecutor Wraith asked the attractive woman on the stand.

She replied. "Amy Walters, I am a registered nurse."

"Are you a full-time employee of Switzer Memorial Hospital?

"No, I am not."

"Would you tell the Court your association with Switzer?"

"I am available as a fill-in nurse, part-time when needed. At times I am hired as a private nurse in the hospital."

"Were you called in to Switzer on February 5, 1964 and in what capacity?"

"Yes, I am by specialty a surgical nurse. I was called in because they were expecting a number of surgical patients."

"Who called you? Dr. Benjamin Bradley?"

"No, the head of the nursing staff, Monica Tines, called me."

"It is my understanding you stayed the two days during this emergency. Is that right?"

"Yes."

"That was commendable, Mrs. Walters. My question to you is, did you work with Dr. Benjamin Bradley all that time?"

"Yes, I did."

"Do you know Dr. Benjamin Bradley outside of the medical profession?"

"Yes."

"How do you know him?"

"My husband and he have been friends for years, even before I met my husband. Ben was my husband's best man at our wedding."

"Is your husband in the courtroom today?"

"No, he's not."

"Why not?"

"Because he is wheel chair bound due to a spinal injury he sustained in an automobile accident a few years ago. He doesn't like to be in the public eye anymore. He was a very good doctor."

"I see, so he is not practicing medicine anymore?"

"No, he's working on a medical research project."

"Now in the very early morning of February 7 around one, one thirty that morning you were in Dr. Benjamin Bradley's office on the seventh floor. The door to his office suite was wide open, as was the door to his inner office. Is that right?"

"I guess so. I don't recall."

"Did you say to Dr. Benjamin Bradley, 'Ben, I could make you incredibly happy, probably far better than Jane can or does?'"

"I don't know what I said. I was extremely tired by then. I don't remember much about that morning, except I wanted to go home and sleep."

"You were heard to say that by someone outside Dr. Benjamin Bradley's office. Are you denying you said that?"

"As I said before, I don't recall much of that early morning including that time in his office."

Prosecutor Wraith decided he could bide his time with Amy Walters for now, and said, "No further questions."

"Mr. Adams?" the judge called.

"No questions for now."

"I call Polly Fields to the stand."

"Your name and occupation?" Prosecutor Wraith asked.

"Polly Fields, I am medical secretary by trade. I was Dr Benjamin Bradley's receptionist."

"How long were you in that position?"

196

"I was hired a couple of weeks after Dr. Bradley took an office suite in the Switzer's section of doctors' offices."

"So you have been with him for many years, almost from the beginning of his private practice?"

"Yes."

"Since you had been with him from the beginning of his private practice, would you say you had come to know him pretty well?"

"Yes."

"Would you say you liked him?"

"Yes, he was a good boss and I respected him."

"When he hired you, Miss Fields, was he married at the time?"

"Yes, he was. His wife's name was Luanne."

"In your opinion what was his first wife like?"

"Well, she was very beautiful, very sophisticated yet personable, pleasant. A woman other women would want to imitate."

"From your observation, would you say Dr. Bradley and his wife Luanne were on amicable terms?"

"Yes, I think so. They appeared to be."

"Would you like to elaborate on that, Miss Fields?"

"Well, for example the doctors' wives host a holiday ball, a formal dinner and dance every year. Sometimes it's held before Christmas and some years on New Year's Eve."

"Late one New Year's Eve afternoon Mrs. Bradley swooped into the office dressed in a lovely gown and carrying Dr. Bradley's tuxedo. He still had a few patients to see before he was done for the day, and so she went into his private office to leave the tuxedo, and then she pulled up a chair next to my desk and chatted with me until all the patients had left. She came so she could save him some steps and time and he wouldn't feel rushed. I think that showed her concern for him. I remember that day very well as it was the last time she attended a Holiday Ball," she added.

"Why was it the last Ball she attended?"

"She died the following winter."

"After her death what was Dr. Bradley like?"

"My guess was he was grieving. I think he was lost without her and just wanted to bury himself in more work. So, when he was asked by the retiring hospital administrator if he could recommend Dr. Bradley to the Board for that position he must have said yes, because the Board made him the hospital administrator."

"Then could it be said Dr. Bradley was quite busy with both his practice and his position with the hospital?"

"Yes."

"What about his social life in the years following his first wife's death?"

"He didn't date that anyone knew of for more than ten years after his wife died. However, I think it was during the third year after her death that some of the doctors' wives convinced him he should attend the Christmas Ball even if he didn't have a date."

"Then he did attend?"

"Yes, he did."

"Did he tell you about his going to the Christmas Ball, Miss Fields?"

"No, my mother and I always make a reservation for dinner at the Durham where the Holiday Balls are held, and on the same day so we can see the ladies in their fineries and the gentlemen in their tuxedos, and watch them dance."

"We saw him sit out the dances and visit with his colleagues and their wives."

"When did you first learn he had married again?"

"The first day Jane began her Pediatrics Residency on Orientation Day. I guess the whole hospital learned that day."

"And how did you feel about that?"

"Well, I was shocked, surprised just like everyone else."

"Were you surprised when he told you he was going to Chicago?"

"Yes."

"And were you curious as to why he decided to spend the whole week in Chicago, instead of a couple of days as first he mentioned?"

"Yes, and when he called me and said he wanted me to arrange his schedule so he could take the whole month of June and the first week of July off, and to tell the board members on the Pediatric Residency Program to be prepared for interviewing the last week in May. I was very surprised since he hadn't taken any time off in, I guess about a dozen years," she offered.

"Did you ask him why he wanted a month off or where he planned to go?"

"No, I didn't. After all, Dr. Bradley was calling long distance and besides, I didn't think he'd appreciate my asking."

"What was your first impression of Jane Bradley when you met her?"

"To be honest, I compared her to Dr. Bradley's first wife. I thought she lacked sophistication, she appeared to be much younger than Dr. Bradley, she was of average looks, and not beautiful like his first wife, and I wondered why she was attracted to him or he to her."

"As time went by, did you think differently of Jane Bradley?"

"Yes, I thought she was immodest at the very least, cheap at best."

"That's pretty harsh, Miss Fields. Why did you think that?"

"She appeared to be always touching Dr. Bradley, teasing him I think."

"Are you saying she acted differently towards him than his first wife did?"

"Yes, definitely, not very respectful of him."

"Did she do this touching in public in front of others?"

"I'm not sure."

"In front of you?"

"No."

"Then how is it Miss Fields, you saw her doing these things?"

"Well one day she came in around lunchtime with their lunch and went into his private office, and waited for him there. When he was finished seeing his patients he joined her in his office. He had left the door slightly ajar; that's how I saw her in action, one might say."

"How much ajar?"

"An inch and an half, two inches, maybe."

"Where is his office?"

"It is half way along the hallway on the left after the double doors leading to the examining rooms."

"If it was lunchtime, why were you in the area of the examining rooms?"

"Because we have a little lounge at the far end of the hallway where we usually have lunch. There is a complete kitchenette, and a radio in that room. Oh, and a window that looks out and beyond the parking area, a very pleasant room."

"If you were heading to the far end of the hallway wouldn't the couple hear you?"

"No, the hallway is carpeted."

"So, what did you see that made you think she lacked sophistication and respect for her husband."

"She was sitting on his desk and he was standing in front of her. He unbuttoned her lab coat. Then while he kissed her, his hand was all over the front of her. Then I saw her hand reach inside his lab coat, I couldn't tell where her hand went. I could only guess."

The prosecutor did not dare risk a look at the jury or to the people sitting in the courtroom. He surmised they were probably enjoying the scandalous account. Looking straight at the witness, he kept his expression under controlled as he continued his questioning.

"Miss Fields, have you ever been married?"

"No, I have not."

"Have any gentlemen friends?"

"Of course I have."

"Do you understand that Benjamin and Jane Bradley are married to each other?"

"Yes, certainly."

"Then do you understand that husbands and wives have every right to ..." He stopped and cleared his throat " to be intimate, personal, to touch one another? Do you understand what I'm trying to say?"

"I believe I do."

"Then what you just described is not really wrong for them. In fact I would say it was wrong of you to watch them, spy on them, so to speak."

"I was not spying on them. I was shocked at what I saw, so shocked I just couldn't move on. After that, my opinion of her went further downhill.

"Frankly, I couldn't help notice how she seemed to tempt him with her touching him, and the way she walked. Come to think of it, she did not present herself well in that area in public."

"How was that?"

"It was the first year she came, that year it was the New Year's Eve Ball."

"My mother made our reservations for that evening as usual. Our table was upstairs, the gallery it's called where the diners can look down on the main level and watch the diners and dancers there. We had an excellent view of the dance floor and the people attending the ball.

"We saw them come in, she was wearing a gown with the bodice cut so low my mother whispered to me, 'If she bends over they are going to fall out!'" Behind the prosecutor there was some muffled laughter that stopped as soon as the witness continued. "Then my mother said a little later, 'No wonder she got pregnant so soon after they were married. She teases him.'"

"I reminded my mother, I had told her some time ago, there were some rumors she was pregnant before they were married, and that he had been shacking up with her in Chicago, and that's why he extended his stay there. My mother said it wouldn't surprise her if that were true after seeing her with Dr. Bradley."

The prosecutor worked at keeping a sly grin from crossing his face as he continued with the cross-examination. "Now," he said, "is that all, Miss Fields, that made you think even less of Dr. Jane Bradley?"

"One more thing. When they first started dancing he danced her into a dark corner that we could see into clearly. We saw him kiss her with one arm around her shoulder and his other hand circling her belly.

"Don't you see, how disgusting, how embarrassing of both of them. Here is a man highly respected all around this area, pawing his wife in public and she by virtue of just being a doctor is granted respect, but ignores good breeding in public.

"Frankly, I was embarrassed for both of them."

"I see."

"You know I tried to overlook all that after their children were born. I even offered to help them."

"Oh, and what did you offer, Miss Fields?"

"Well, it was after the second boy was born, less than a year after the first one! Well, Dr. Bradley and I were sitting in the office lounge and I brought him the mail that came in that morning. There was a piece of mail that was of interest to him. I think I saw his eyes light up when he read it. Naturally, I was curious, but I didn't say anything. Then he picked up the phone and called his home. He didn't seem to be concerned that I was sitting there. He told his wife he was holding an invitation to a two-day meeting for Hospital Administrators in New York City the following month. He wanted her to go with him."

"Apparently she was concerned about leaving the children. He said 'I'll find someone we can leave them

202

with.' Well, I didn't offer to baby sit just then, but I was thinking if she goes with Dr. Bradley to the City, she'll probably come back pregnant, again!" Polly Fields hesitated long enough to let her last statement resonate in the courtroom and have her meaning understood before moving on.

"In any case," she went on, "I told my mother that night. She thought it would be nice if she and I took care of the children. After all, Dr. Bradley was very attentive to my mother in the hospital following the emergency surgery she underwent some time ago. In fact he stopped in to see her a few times at home after she was discharged. Dr. Bradley makes house calls from time to time to see how his patients are doing.

"My mother thought it would be a way we could express our appreciation for his kindness. So the next day, I made our offer to baby sit. He thanked me, and said he would tell his wife about my offer.

"She called me the next day and thanked me for offering, but had decided she really wasn't ready to leave the baby, so if she was going, she would take both children.

"I hated to tell my mother she said no because my mother was excited over the prospect of having babies in the house. But my mother said she could understand Jane not wanting to leave the baby. Frankly I felt bad for my mother."

"I see. Did you consider that a rejection on the part of Jane Bradley and hold it against her?

"Of course not, everything I have told you has been the absolute truth no matter how it reflects on anyone!"

"I appreciate that, Miss Fields. Now I need to ask you, did you have, or do you have romantic feelings towards Benjamin Bradley?"

Surprised at the sudden change in subject, "No, of course not," she answered quickly and sounding indignant.

"You never dated Dr. Bradley?"

Polly hesitated. By her tortured-looking facial expressions she appeared to be caught in a difficult situation. Onlookers, surprised too by the question, wondered how far these scandalous revelations could go.

"Well," she began slowly, "it was the October before he married, and we were in the lounge having lunch. Like all the doctors' offices in that building, we were closed from noon until one except for emergencies. Besides the radio there is a telephone and of course we can hear pages. So emergencies and pages are answered during the lunch hour.

"I always brought my morning newspaper in the lounge during lunch. Dr. Bradley liked the Sports section and would snatch that up as soon as I put the papers on the table, whenever he had lunch in the lounge. Then he would sit back lost completely in that section and eat while he read. The last page in that section is the listing of the local entertainment, as everyone probably knows. Anyway, I heard him suddenly exclaimed, 'Wow, look at that!' I put down my paper and asked, 'Look at what?'"

"He read aloud the advertisement that had caught his attention. 'Every first Saturday of October the Starlight Drive In offers triple features for the price of one dollar per car, as an annual thank you to our customers for their patronage during the season and to say we are closing until next spring, after the triple feature.

Do you know who are in the triple features this year?" he asked.

"I have no idea,' I said."

"Ma and Pa Kettle, Dean Martin and Jerry Lewis and my all-time favorite, Abbot and Costello. What a line up! I'll be there rain or snow! Do you go to the drive-in, Polly?" he asked me.

'I used to go on occasion a long time ago,' I said.

"It's great entertainment; fresh air, popcorn, candy, soft drinks, good movies and all in the comfort of your car. Oh, and sometimes in the summer you can swat the mosquitoes while you're watching the movies and not bother anyone.

If you wanted to get reacquainted with drive-in entertainment Saturday night would be the time. I park in the back, the far end of the last row before the concession stand. Best spot in the house!'"

"Just then there was a page for Dr. Bradley and he left after answering it so I didn't get a chance to respond."

"That Saturday, I went to the drive-in and parked next to his car. He was headed into the concession stand when I pulled in. So, as soon as I parked I followed him in. He happened to turn around in the line and saw me and started talking to me. He asked what I wanted, and bought my popcorn and soda pop. We walked back to the cars and he invited me to sit with him. I did."

"Would you consider that a date, Miss Fields?"

"I'm not sure."

"Did he make any advances toward you during the movies?"

"No."

"Did he kiss you good night?"

"No."

"Did he suggest he might call you for a date?"

"No."

"Then that was all you knew of him socially?"

There was a pause so long that the judge asked her to respond to the question.

Still she said nothing.

The prosecutor asked again. "Perhaps you didn't understand the question, Miss Fields." Her eyes had a strange faraway look in them, and the prosecutor was thinking the prim and proper Miss Fields was now in a trap and would soon ...

"Except the night I slept with him," she broke into his thoughts.

Shocked gasps resounded throughout the courtroom. But no shocked looks were greater than those of Dr. Benjamin Franklin Bradley. Stunned, Bradley's mouth dropped opened.

It was obvious by the look on the prosecutor's face that he too was shock by this unexpected revelation. It took a few seconds for the prosecutor to regain his composure so that he could ask, "Would you tell the court about that night? When did this occur?"

Polly drew in a deep breath then slowly let it out. "When she was in the hospital as a patient after the accident."

"Miss Fields, are you telling the Court that you and Dr. Benjamin Bradley slept together while his wife was in the hospital?"

"Yes," she stated flatly.

"Frankly, Miss Fields, I find that hard to believe. Would you tell this court about that time?"

"I had offered to stay with his children in the evenings after work, and stay through the night. This was when she was first admitted in the hospital. But, Dr. Bradley said no thank you, he and the boys would be staying in her room. He said he wouldn't leave her alone.

"It was about a month later when I heard Dr. Bradley had decided to let the boys stay home with their regular babysitter, Mrs. Mellon. And that he was home at night because his wife was recovering, and she didn't think he was getting enough rest in the hospital.

"One day he asked me if I would drop something off to his children at lunchtime, while he went to the hospital in Overlook. That's where she was recovering.

"Mrs. Stewart, their housekeeper, was there. She let me in to give the gift, the boys' father had gotten for them. It was a log building set of some sort. The boys took the boxes into the living room to play with, and Mrs. Stewart asked if I'd like some tea. I said yes, and asked if I could use the bathroom. She pointed out the one in the hallway, in the bedroom area, because she said that was all cleaned. She went into the kitchen, I went into the bedroom area and looked for their room."

"Whose room, Miss Fields?"

"Dr. Bradley's and his wife's bedroom."

"Why did you want to see their bedroom?"

"I was just curious.

"The door was open so I walked in. It is a very big room. There is a bathroom and a huge walk-in closet in that room. But what was more impressive is they have an unusually big bed. It's very long and wide and high off the floor. They have a bed skirt around it. In fact I got down on the floor to see if someone could crawl under the bed. I discovered that one could actually lie comfortably under the bed.

"I went back into the kitchen. Mrs. Stewart had made some tea and had set the table with some little cakes to go with the tea. When we sat down we chatted like ladies do over a cup of tea, and I learned a lot about the Bradley family from her."

"What did you learn, Miss Fields?" the prosecutor asked

"It seems she is more of the discipliner of the boys than Dr. Bradley is. She doesn't like yellow roses. Mrs. Stewart thought it was because she knew that yellow roses were Luanne Bradley's favorite colored roses. Anyway, when she first moved in, she had some landscaping done that included roses. She made it clear to the landscaper she did not want yellow roses. Because all of the walls in the house were white she had some rooms painted in different colors, and again she said no yellow colors on the walls. I gathered that Mrs. Stewart had been with Dr. and Mrs. Benjamin Bradley ever since they moved to Glenwood. It seems Mrs. Stewart thinks well of Dr. Bradley's second wife.

"In any case, I decided right then I would sleep there that night. I asked Mrs. Stewart if she would be baby-sitting that night. She said no, Mrs. Mellon would be there. I said I would be willing to stay with the children this evening if that would help. Mrs. Stewart said that would be nice since both she and her sister, Mrs. Mellon, had been alternating nights and weekends."

207

"I told her I could be there at 4:30 PM. She said she would have a supper cooking by the time I got there. Also Dr. Bradley has dinner with his wife and usually doesn't come home until around 9 PM.

"That night he came home shortly after nine. He looked so tired. He was surprised to see me there. I explained how I was giving a break to Mrs. Mellon and how she was appreciative. That satisfied him. I offered to make some tea, and he accepted my offer. In the meantime, he left the kitchen and went in to see his children who were asleep in their room."

"Later, he and I sat at the kitchen table drinking tea and chatting. He said Jane was doing well, and he hoped to bring her home soon, sooner than she expected. Then he asked me about his surgical schedule for the next day and reminded me to coordinate his private practice schedule with Marsha , his secretary in the Administrator's Office. I assured him I would. When he finished his tea, he said he was going to take a shower and go to bed."

"I immediately said 'Go ahead, I'll just pick up and see myself out.' He thanked me and left the kitchen. I picked up and waited a few minutes before I headed down the hallway. I noticed he had left the children's room door ajar, as he did his bedroom door. I listened in the hallway and heard the shower running. Cautiously, I went into his bedroom and checked to see if the bathroom door was open; it was not. I stepped into the room and quickly looked around before I slipped under the bed."

There was a triumphant glimmer in her eyes that made those who could see it uneasy. "I had put my coat, handbag, shoes and boots in a paper shopping bag and hid them behind a bush beside the front door right after I finished picking up the kitchen. I did that so if I had to leave in a hurry, I could easily get my things and be quickly away. I had parked my car a short way up from the Doctor's house.

"Under the bed, I took off my dress and rolled it and placed it on the floor near the top of the bed. Again in case

I needed to get it in a hurry. Now that I was ready, I crawled over to the other side of the bed and lifted up the bed skirt in front of me so I had a good view of the bathroom door."

"It was a long while before Dr. Bradley came out of his bathroom. He left a light on in the bathroom and in that streak of light behind him I could see him clearly. He had on a towel and nothing else. I noticed he is fat and hairy."

The sound of the judge's gavel stopped Polly. "We don't need any more description of Dr. Bradley, Miss Fields," he warned.

The prosecutor looked at Polly Fields and wondered again how long it would be before the meaning of this whole trial would come to light. "Now, Miss Field, what happened next?"

"I was surprised to see him kneel down beside his bed and talk to God. Do you want to know what he said?"

After a moment, the prosecutor answered in the affirmative and Polly Fields continued, "He started with thanking God that Jane had survived and then he asked God to help him to be patient as she healed. That was about it."

"Then he got into bed and fell asleep. I waited a long time until I was sure he was asleep before I crawled out from under the bed and into the bed. It was a while later when Dr. Bradley started taking in his sleep and moving towards me. 'Jane!' he called. 'Honey, cuddle up to me. I didn't get married to sleep alone.'

"I was certain he was sound asleep, but I wanted to get out of bed and go home before he realized I was there, but just as I was about to move the telephone rang. Out of panic I carefully but quickly slipped out of the sheets and back under the bed when he moved away towards the telephone.

"I was amazed how alert he sounded when he picked up the handset. 'Dr. Bradley,' he answered. It was his wife. He was obviously very worried about her by the sound of his voice. The first thing he asked her was she all right? I guessed she was crying because he spoke in a soft soothing tone and was telling her she would be all right. I guessed she may have been concerned about her mood from what he was saying. Dr. Bradley told her he had been dreaming she was in bed with him now and how he was disappointed she wasn't. Then he said he would bundle up the boys and the three of them would stay with her that night. The conversation lasted quite a few minutes and I guess she told him that going to the hospital wasn't necessary. He ended the conversation by telling her he loved her and that she would be fine and he would see her the next day.

"A couple of minutes later the phone rang again. He answered as usual, and I heard him sound quite surprised when he addressed the caller, Marjorie. Needless to say I was curious as to who was this Marjorie. After a while from the conversation I understood it was his wife's mother I gathered from his repeating of what she said, his wife's parents would be arriving the next day. Dr. Bradley sounded happy they were coming and he promised to pick them up at the airport the next day.

"It couldn't have been more than a couple of minutes later one of his sons called out to him. In a flash, he was out of the bed and over to his dresser. I heard him ruffling in his dresser, and when I lifted up the bed skirt I could see he was quickly putting on some pajamas. Then he left the room. I couldn't hear what he was saying to his little boy while he was in the boys' room, but I heard him talking to one of the boys as they were crossing the hallway into Dr. Bradley's room. I lifted up the bed skirt and I saw him carrying one of the boys and the other one was walking beside him holding his father's hand. He said to the boys as they neared the bed, 'You two sleep here tonight. Mommy will be home tomorrow, so you will sleep in your own beds tomorrow, and your grandparents will be here too, and they will sleep in the room next to yours. There is nothing to be afraid of. I'm here and I won't let anything hurt you two.'

210

"Apparently, not only does Dr. Bradley snore but so do his little boys. Sometime later I heard all three of them snoring so I thought it was safe to leave. I literally crawled out of that bedroom and into the hallway before I got up and ran into the hallway leading to the front door. I gathered up my shopping bag from behind the bush and ran to my car. How embarrassing! I felt like a thief!"

The prosecutor decided this was not the time to spring some pertinent information on the court. So he announced, "No more questions, Miss Fields."

"Mr. Adams?" the judge addressed the defense attorney.

"I have no questions at this time."

Chapter 22 - The Trial Part Two

The prosecutor then called, "I call Dr. Benjamin Franklin Bradley to the stand."

Once Bradley was sworn in the prosecutor immediately went on the attack.

"Dr. Bradley, you heard Miss Fields testimony?"

"Yes."

"You heard me ask if she had any romantic feelings towards you?"

"Yes, I did."

"Now, I ask you, did you or do you have any romantic feelings towards Miss Fields?"

Shocked, Dr. Bradley answered in an angry tone, "Of course not!"

"Is it possible you developed romantic feelings towards another woman and had hatched this plan to kill your wife in such a way as to make it look like an accident?"

Bradley was now angrier than before. "How dare you suggest anything like that? I love my wife, she is the mother of my children, I am loyal to her!!!"

"Your Honor, I believe Dr. Bradley is at the moment a hostile witness, and I would like to excuse him for now and will call my next witness."

"You may step down, Dr. Bradley," the judge said.

No sooner had Benjamin stepped down than the prosecutor called out, "I call Dr. Jane Bradley to the stand."

Wraith began his line of questioning right after Jane was sworn in. "Dr. Bradley, what was your first impression of your husband when you met him in Chicago?."

"Well, his back was to me. I saw he was very tall and I thought he must be quite old because his hair, while thick, was white. Later he told me his hair began turning gray in high school and was all white by the time he entered medical school. So, he isn't really old,." she added.

"Did you hear Miss Fields' testimony?"

"Yes, I did and may I state here and now I was not pregnant when Ben and I were married, and furthermore, we did not sleep together while he was in Chicago. I lived in the student nurses' dorm when I was an intern. You can be sure the house mothers would have frowned on his sleeping in my room."

"I think you've made that perfectly clear, Dr. Bradley. Now will you tell the Court, was it you or your husband that didn't want Miss Fields to baby-sit your children or stay in your home?"

"It was me."

"Why?"

"I sensed she didn't like me and I thought her being in our home would make me feel like a stranger in my own home. And of course, I didn't want my children to feel out of place in their home either. Those were my only reasons for not wanting her to baby-sit."

"Do you think your husband had romantic feelings toward Miss Fields?"

"No, I doubt it."

"Why not?"

"Because she is a highly-qualified, respected and trustworthy employee in his eyes and that's all."

"Do you think Dr. Bradley, as a woman, that Miss Fields had or has romantic feelings towards your husband?"

"I think it's possible."

"Is it possible you think that Miss Fields had hostile feelings towards you?"

"I didn't think she liked me, but I don't think she had hostile feelings towards me."

"Dr. Jane Bradley, are you aware your accident was not an accident but a carefully planned attempt to murder you?"

"I have been told that."

"Thank you, Dr. Bradley. No more questions."

"Mr. Adams?"

"No questions at this time."

"Your Honor, I'd like to call Sergeant Liston to the stand."

"Sergeant Liston, you are with the State Police stationed at the G Troop Barracks on Hover Hill?"

"Yes, sir, I am."

"Did you respond to the accident on Route 18 South in the early hours of February eighth, 1964?"

"Yes, sir, my partner and I did."

"Can you tell the court what you saw when you arrived at the scene?"

"Yes, there were two snow plow trucks parked perpendicular to the edge of the road with their high beams directed into a small field.

"The two drivers were at the crash site when we got there. The car was upside down in the snow. We saw a figure lying in a heap, over on the passenger side. It looked like a woman. She wasn't moving; we assumed she was unconscious. The men had called for an ambulance and it arrived minutes after we did. It took all of us to pry her car door off to get the lady out of the car. She had to be carried from the car across the field to the road, where the ambulance was parked. We did not know for sure who she was until we put her in the ambulance. Dr. Jane Bradley is my children's pediatrician.

"Once we had her in the ambulance, I called our dispatcher and told him we would personally notify Dr. Benjamin Bradley and take him to Overlook. That's where the ambulance was taking his wife.

"Before we left , my partner and I sealed off the area. The snow was still coming down fast but my partner thought he could still get some tire marks on film and the position of the car and the deep marks caused by the car as it spun out of control and flipped into the field. So he took out the flash camera and took several pictures, just in case.

"We then drove to Dr. Benjamin Bradley's house. We rang the door bell several times before Dr. Bradley came to the door. When he saw who we were, he looked surprised.

"I said, 'There has been an accident. It's your wife.' He looked shocked. He asked, 'How bad is she?'

"I said, 'We don't know, the ambulance took her to Overlook, because it was closer.'

"'I have to get dressed and get my children up,' he said, as he turned away from us and started moving out of that hallway.

"We followed him."

"'What was she doing out?' I asked.

"'She was called out on an emergency,' he answered.

"'When was that?' My partner asked.

"'About one.'

"'That was almost two hours ago,.' I said.

"'I'll be dressed in a few minutes.' He said as he went into what looked like his bedroom. My partner and I walked across the hallway. I opened wide the door that was ajar and turned on the light. The children were sleeping.

"We waited outside their bedroom. In a few minutes Dr. Bradley came out of his room. 'I have to bring my children,' he said as he went past us.

"He woke them up, put on their bathrobes and socks and slippers and carried both of them out of their room. When they asked where they were going he told them to the hospital to see their mother. One of the boys asked, 'Mommy working?' He didn't respond to the boy. Dr. Bradley walked past the hallway that led to the front door and on into the kitchen. He put the boys down and put on their coats and took his coat from off the hook, and had his hand on the door that went out to the garage.

"Patrick asked 'Where are you going, Doc?'

"'I'm going to get my car. I have to drive us down to the hospital.'

"'No, doc, we're going to drive you down. It's still snowing out.'

"Patrick picked up the younger boy and took the hand of the older boy. It looked as though Dr. Bradley was not thinking. I put my hand on Dr. Bradley's shoulder and

215

guided him in the other direction. It was Patrick's and my opinion that Dr. Bradley was in shock.

"Once we were in the hospital, we found arrangements had already been made for a nurse to take the children and stay with them in an unoccupied room. We learned later that the charge nurse in the ER had called the Overlook Hospital Administrator, Mr. Harris, and told him about the accident. He had anticipated the Bradley family's needs and gave instructions for them before he headed to the hospital. Mr. Harris met us in the ER. There was a nurse waiting with him to take the children.

"Dr. Bradley asked where the nurse was taking them. After he heard, he kissed the boys and told them to be good. One of the boys asked 'Where is Mommy?' Before Dr. Bradley could answer, Mr. Harris answered,. 'She is with the doctors.'

"Dr. Bradley watched as the nurse took the boys by the hand and into the elevator with Patrick beside them.

"We were escorted to the surgical waiting room. A nurse happened to come out of surgery just as we got there. She saw us and turned and went back into surgery. A few minutes later Dr. Richardson came out; he walked right up to Dr. Bradley. For the first time Dr. Bradley seemed alert when Dr. Richardson sat down across from him. 'Ben, the baby was dead when Jane arrived. I'm sorry. Jane was hemorrhaging; we removed her uterus. She has a concussion. We took care of the most serious problems, but we're going to have to watch her.'

"Dr. Bradley nodded his head, he understood. Just then the door opened, and a nurse and Dr. David Morgan came through. Dr. Morgan was guiding a hospital bassinet. There was a blanket covering a small body in the bassinet.

"Dr. Morgan stopped when he saw Dr. Bradley. Dr. Bradley stood up and walked the few steps to the bassinet and asked, 'My baby?'

"'Yes, Ben,' Dr. Morgan answered, and then added, 'A little girl, Ben, do you want to name her?'

216

"As Doctor Morgan spoke, Dr. Bradley lifted the blanket away from the baby's face. 'Name her Emily Jane Bradley, Emily after my mother and Jane, after her mother.'

"'All right Ben, I'll make sure it's on the death certificate. I'll be back up after we bring her down to the morgue.'

"Something he said seemed to bring Dr. Bradley out of shock because he said, 'I don't want my child cremated. I will arrange a proper burial for her with the Granger Funeral Home.'"

"What happened next?"

"He watched Dr. Morgan and the nurse go. Once they were out of sight he walked over to the window and stared out. From where I was, I could see one side of his face. He was very quiet but I saw tears roll down his cheek.

"Dr. Richardson and Mr. Harris were quietly talking together. I couldn't hear what they were saying, but I saw Dr. Richardson shake his head, agreeing with Mr. Harris.

"About this time my partner came in. He went over to Dr. Bradley and told him where his children were and that they were asleep. I heard Dr. Bradley thank him. Then Dr. Bradley did something unexpected. I was standing when he came over to me and thanked me for coming to the house and bringing him and his children to the hospital. We shook hands, and he turned to Patrick and shook his hand, and thanked him again. We wished him well and hoped that his wife would recover soon, and if he needed our help to call us. After that we left."

"Did you speak to Dr. Jane Bradley at a later date?"

"Yes, we called the hospital two weeks later to find out if Dr. Jane Bradley had regained consciousness so we could question her."

"And, did you talk to her?"

"Yes, but what she said didn't make sense. Apparently she thought she was hit by something from behind her."

"Was she any help in naming who hit her?"

"No, she didn't seem to remember much of that night."

"Thank you, Sergeant Liston, no more questions."

"Mr. Adams?"

"No questions for now."

For the time being, Wraith had his reasons for not bringing up the physical evidence against an individual present in the court room.

After dismissing Sergeant Liston from the witness stand, the judge called for a lunch recess until one thirty that afternoon.

While Jane wanted to bolt from the courtroom when recess was called, Benjamin instead held her back to wait until the courtroom was empty and said to her, "I'm glad our children are too young to be here, or understand what's going on. I never thought we would be thrown naked into a scandalous whirlpool.

"I feel like we are drowning in a nightmare while a crowd that is fully dressed is watching us drown," he added.

"Jane, I've been thinking we should consider selling everything we have and move somewhere else outside of New York, and start over for our sakes and our sons' sakes." Ben had been holding Jane's hand all the while, and as he spoke he gripped her hand with the strength of a determined younger man."

"Yes, Ben," she sighed," I'd like to leave as soon as possible. Maybe to Indiana?"

"We'll see," he said.

At the time the Bradley's were unaware a big burly gentleman was behind them, and listening intently to everything they were saying. "Excuse me, Dr. Bradley."

Benjamin turned around to see who had spoken to him. He stood up with a smile, and extended his hand as he greeted the listener. "Thomas, how are you?." he asked as the two shook hands.

"I'm well, thanks to you, Dr. Bradley."

218

Benjamin smiled. "I always like hearing that. Thanks Thomas. Does my ego good."

Turning to Jane and then back to Thomas, "Thomas, let me introduce you to my wife, Jane Bradley."

The bailiff reached across Benjamin to shake Jane's hand. A close look into Jane's eyes, and he could see why Benjamin was in love with her. "It's a pleasure to meet you, Dr. Bradley."

"Same here," she said and asked, "Out of curiosity, how do you know my husband?"

"He saved my life when I was younger. I had bleeding ulcers. Once he took care of my ulcer problem, he encouraged me to leave my job and find another. I was a bouncer at the Spider's Place in Tinker Town. Your husband suggested I look into this job; said he'd be a reference for me. He kept his word and I got the job."

"That's nice to hear." Jane's smile expanded as she looked at Thomas and back again to Benjamin.

Thomas glanced back and to the far side of the courtroom. He spotted the man he had been waiting for. "Well, how about lunch? Let me show you the back door to this building."

Benjamin and Jane followed Thomas to a door in a far corner in front of the courtroom. To their surprise, on the other side of the door, Sergeant Liston was waiting.

Liston began, "It's busy out front, so we decided there would be less commotion if we took you out the back way."

Just as Liston was about to escort the Bradley's out the door, Thomas said, "By the way, Liston, seems Dr. Bradley is thinking of taking his family and moving away from here. Thought that might be of interest to you."

"Thanks, Thomas, it is," Liston responded.

Benjamin and Jane were escorted to an unmarked car. Sergeant Liston's partner, Patrick Burton, was behind the wheel. Twenty minutes later the car pulled into a diner on

219

the edge of Tinker Town. "We managed to have a table reserved for us," Burton announced.

"Food must be good; there are a lot of cars here," Jane observed.

"It's good and it's reasonable," Liston said.

Inside, the troopers sat across the table from the couple. Liston said, "To save time we ordered today's special in advance."

Jane smiled, "This could be interesting."

"Thomas said you are looking to move out of here," Liston began.

"Yes," Benjamin replied.

"Why?" Burton asked.

Benjamin looked at the two troopers. "Were you both in the courtroom from the beginning of this trial?"

"Yes," Burton answered for both of them.

"Then you must have heard the testimony of my receptionist."

Their looks told him they had heard so he went on. "I was taught, gentlemen and ladies do not discuss intimate behavior unless it's with their spouse. Nor do polite people expound on other people's state of undress. I can't believe Jane and I were subjected to that humiliation. We don't deserve that.

"Since I opened my practice in this area I have tried to be civic-minded. I have been the physician for both towns' high school football and basketball teams and never asked for compensation. I have taught emergency procedures for injuries and survival skills to you troopers, the local fire departments and local police departments and charged no fees.

"Yet, my wife is almost killed, vicious gossip is repeated and the intimate details of our life are paraded in front of a packed court room, and you wonder why I want to move my family from this area? I don't understand the reasoning behind the questions nor can I glean anything from the answers."

Liston responded, "Doc, there are good reasons for the questions being asked. Just be patient and you'll see why the questions."

"Sweetheart, surely the worse is over," Jane tried to reassure her husband.

At the sound of the judge's gavel, the court came to order. The prosecutor called his first witness of the afternoon, "Mr. Matt Hunter."

The Bradley's were surprised. They had no idea Hunter was in the courtroom or that he was to testify.

Prosecutor Wraith began. "Now, Mr. Hunter I understand you represent Architectural Designs, the company that will design the proposed Medical Research Center in Glenwood. Is that correct?"

"I am not a representative of the Company in its truest sense, I am one of the firm's architects."

"You have won several awards for your designs here and abroad. Is that right?"

"Yes."

"Then how is it you came to a sleepy town like Glenwood to propose a design for a medical research center?"

"It's good business to offer to design buildings everywhere. But I am not involved in looking for prospective projects. At times I am asked to attend meetings with the sales people to help them with questions."

"Before you came, did you know the Bradleys?"

"No, I did not know the Bradleys before I came here."

"You do understand you are under oath, Mr. Hunter?"

"Yes, I know, and I repeat I did not know the Bradleys before I came here. You need to ask that question differently in order to get the answer you are looking for."

"All right, Mr. Hunter, did you know Jane Bradley but not by the name Bradley?"

"Yes."

221

"Would you tell the court how you met her and what was your relationship to her?"

Matt began, "I met Jane at a Saturday afternoon matinee in Chicago. At the last minute the lady I had invited to attend the play with me was unable to attend. I had purchased two tickets. As I waited to go into the theater, I noticed an attractive young woman step up to the ticket booth. I guessed she had asked how much for a ticket, because she stepped back out of the line and fished in her wallet. I noticed she was even counting coins. It was obvious she didn't have enough money to pay for a ticket, as she turned around and was headed towards the door.

"I intercepted her and explained I had two tickets and my date couldn't come. I offered to give her one. She refused to accept a free ticket, but asked me how much I would sell it to her for. We agreed on a price and she paid it. Since I couldn't use the ticket, I sold it for less than what it cost me. Naturally, her seat was next to mine, so we talked before the curtain went up and during intermission, and after the play, I invited her to dine with me at a nearby restaurant.

"It wasn't long afterwards; we started to date. Frankly, I was in love with her.

"Towards the end of her internship I had to leave for Germany. I had asked her to come with me and do her residency there. She said no to that, and no to my marriage proposal. So when we said goodbye at the airport, I thought I would never see her again.

"I didn't see her again until she walked into the Conference room at Switzer Memorial Hospital. I had no idea she had married Benjamin Bradley, or that she had two sons by him. After our meeting with her husband, I looked for her office. She made it clear she had nothing to do with the project, and would not attempt to influence her husband in the matter. I explained to her I was not looking to her

222

for help in securing the bid. When I asked her to have coffee with me she said no. Basically, that was it."

"Did you ask her if her husband knew of you, and the relationship between the two of you?"

"That came up."

"And her answer was?"

"Yes, she had told him about me."

Some people in the courtroom wondered if the prosecutor was looking for another motive that would connect Benjamin Bradley in the attempted murder of his wife.

"You came here with two others from your firm, your first trip here, did you not?" It seemed the prosecutor had suddenly changed direction in his line of questioning.

"Yes, I did," Hunter answered.

"The three of you were here for two days. The first day you three met with Dr. Benjamin Bradley as chairman of the research center project?"

"Yes."

"The second day the three of you met with Dr. Bradley and with the Research Center Board?"

"Yes."

"After the first meeting, the three of you went back to your hotel. But you took the rental car and went somewhere. Where was that, Mr. Hunter?"

"I looked in the phone book for Jane's address, and drove to her house."

"Why?"

"I'm an architect and I was curious as to the style of house she lived in. I wasn't surprised to see she lived in an el-shaped ranch. I guessed it would be easier for Jane to take care of, and keep an eye on her children. I would have been very surprised if she lived in a palatial mansion. I didn't think that would be Jane's style."

"So, you knew where she lived?"

"Yes."

"Did you let her know you were in her neighborhood?"

"No."

"Why not?"

"It would not be appropriate. Jane obviously has a deep love for her husband and their marriage. She did not want a suggestive shadow on her marriage, or one on mine. In fact, that was her reason for not going to coffee with me."

"You came back to Glenwood by yourself the day before Dr. Jane Bradley's accident. Is that right?"

"Yes."

"Why?"

"Because I wanted to see the area in winter and I had a couple of spare days.

"We came in early spring and I took photos of the area set aside for the new building. I did the same that February because the winter is a dark season and I wanted to be sure I offered a design of the building in such a way that there would be plenty of natural light to help offset the darker days."

The prosecutor went on. "Mr. Hunter, the way I see it Jane Bradley rejected you three times. She said no to marriage, no to going to Germany and no to going out and having coffee with you. That must have hurt. And on top of all that, you saw she is in love with her husband and she had two children by him. You found out where she lived, you could have easily have found out when she was on call and what route she would take to Overlook.

"Since you would have had time to look over the route she would take, you could have easily planned on where to hit her from behind, and send her car over the embankment and into the field. The weather and the road conditions that night made it easier for you to create a possibly fatal accident!"

"You're wrong! I would never consider killing her! Never!" There was no mistaking Matt Hunter's anger at the prosecutor's accusation.

"Mr. Adams?"

"I would like to recall Dr. Jane Bradley to the stand."

224

The courtroom spectators were aghast at the questioning of Matt Hunter and wondered why Wraith did not further question Hunter, or ask more direct questions. And what could Adams ask Jane Bradley that would have a significant bearing on this case?

Adams began, "You want to keep in mind, Dr. Bradley, you are still under oath.

"Approximately two weeks after the accident, in the morning and after you had regained consciousness, your husband was seen sitting on the edge of your bed talking to you. You were crying and were heard to say, "How could you do that to me, Ben?"

"Do you recall saying that?"

"Yes, I remember."

"Would you tell the court what you meant by that?"

Jane took a deep breath before she spoke again. "I had little memory of the accident, but more importantly I had no memory of being pregnant. In fact I wasn't sure why I was in the hospital.

"Ben was explaining everything to me. He was very careful about telling me about the accident. He told me I had been in a car accident and the circumstances, the reason I was out in a storm that night. He asked questions to see what I remembered as he told me about the accident.

"It was the next morning he asked me about our children. I knew them and then he asked me about our baby. I couldn't remember the baby at first. Then slowly the memory of the accident and the fact I was pregnant came to the fore.

"Ben then told me about the arrangements he had made for the baby. He began with describing the white casket for the baby, and then how he bought her a dress and took the hat, the sweater, the booties and the blanket I had knitted for the baby to the funeral parlor to have her dressed in them. He placed a small pink rose in the casket with her.

"It was distressing to hear those details for both of us but what disturbed me the most was that he had our little

225

girl placed in the same mausoleum where his first wife's remains are. I was angry when he told me that. I realized later I was being unreasonable, and I was very sorry I said that to him. It was having our child's remains put in that mausoleum that set me off. And that's when I shouted, 'How could you do that to me, Ben?'

"Ben promised in the spring he would make the arrangements to have her buried in the baby section of the Glenwood Cemetery. He kept his promise."

"Thank you, Dr. Bradley."

Mr. Adams turned to the judge and said, "No more questions."

"Mr. Wraith?"

"No questions for Dr. Jane Bradley, but I would like to recall Miss Polly Fields to the stand, your Honor.

"Miss Fields, you are aware you are still under oath."

"Yes," Polly Fields answered Mr. Wraith.

"Miss Fields, did you know Dr. Jane Bradley was pregnant before the accident?"

"Yes, her pregnancy was very obvious. She was due in March, I believe."

"Now, Miss Fields, supposing you were Dr. Benjamin Bradley's wife what would you do?"

While taken by surprised at that question Polly Fields, seemed to be delighted to answer it. Without hesitation she began, "Well, the first thing I would do would be to find a boarding school for both boys."

"Why?" the prosecutor asked.

"Because Dr. Bradley is forty-seven years old, he can't be running after two little boys. That's too much for a man his age. It's not that he wouldn't see them. They would be home for the holidays and summer vacation.

"Then I would insist we take regular vacations, and have occasional dinner parties. Have a social life for both our sakes. That would be relaxing and good for us, and besides he wouldn't have to worry about my embarrassing him."

"What do you mean, Miss Fields?" Wraith probed.

"Well, let's take the first New Year's Eve Ball they went to. She was pregnant. The next year she was pregnant again, and she wore the same gown to the Ball both years. That must have been embarrassing for him. His first wife never wore the same gown twice to the Balls. Her wearing the same gown made it look like he couldn't provide for a wife. I was so embarrassed for him when I saw her wear the same gown the following year! In fact she wore that same gown for the Christmas Ball that last year, and, of course, she was pregnant again. I'm sure she could have found another gown that would have suited her pregnancy, if she cared about how she looked.

"As his wife, I wouldn't embarrass him like that, nor would I tease him like she does. She just won't leave him alone! You can be sure Luanne wasn't like that. You never saw him put his arm around her in public, like he does with this wife."

"You know, Miss Fields, it sounds as though you really care for Dr. Benjamin Bradley," the prosecutor stated in a slightly condescending tone.

"Well, he's a fine man, he's very caring of his patients and everyone knows he has an excellent reputation as a surgeon. He should be treated with dignity and not burdened. Here Jane was thirty two years old and expecting another baby. I think that would have been too much for him to handle."

"How is it you know their ages?"

"I know Dr. Bradley's age because when I first started to work for him I had to type out some official forms for him, and they needed his birth date. With Jane I looked in her file, her birth date is in there too."

"Why were you looking in her file?"

"I wondered how she got into the Residency Program at Switzer's. Switzer's has very high standards for the Intern and Residency Programs. So I thought, maybe he pulled some strings to get her into the program. You remember I

227

spoke about the rumors that were going around that implied they had to get married. Well, there was only one way to find out if he had pulled strings to get her into the program."

"What did you find out?"

"He apparently didn't. Her academic record was outstanding as were her references, and according to the minutes of her interview the interviewing Board was very impressed with her responses to their questions."

"All that information was in her file?"

"Yes."

"So it seems Jane Bradley earned her admittance to Switzer's Residency Program, and it would be my guess that her husband was proud of her. Would you say that was true Miss Fields?"

Shrugging her shoulders Polly said. "I suppose so."

"The fact is Miss Fields you just don't like Jane Bradley. Is that the way it is?"

"Yes." She answered without hesitation.

"And too Miss Fields you wanted her dead?"

"Yes!" Polly Fields tone was so cold it sent chills down the spines of some of the onlookers.

Prosecutor Wraith continued. "You could easily find out Jane Bradley's on call schedule?"

"Yes." She answered with her now familiar icy tone of voice.

"I suggest Miss Fields that in the first hour of Saturday, February 8, 1964, you made a telephone call from a phone booth on the south side of Overlook to the Bradley residence. You disguised your voice and convinced Dr. Jane Bradley you had a sick child you were bringing to the hospital in Overlook. In that way you lured Dr. Bradley out early on that dark stormy morning. You then headed up to the road you knew she would travel to reach the hospital in Overlook. There you waited until she reached the right spot, and you slammed into the back of her car so hard that it spun out of her control and flipped over the embankment and left her, and the Bradley's unborn child, for dead. I suggest that you wanted her dead badly enough to risk being out in a brewing storm yourself. Is that right Miss Fields?"

"Yes" She hissed. "I wanted her dead that bad. I had thought about it for a long time. But when Friday the storm had begun to weaken I thought I'd have to wait for another storm. Then it was like a sign, as the winds picked up and the snow kept coming long into the night, I knew this was the time to get rid of her. I anticipated everything except the plows. When I heard the baby she was carrying was dead I was glad, and when I learned she was in a coma and in critical condition I had hope."

"You hoped for what Miss Fields?"

"That she would die, then Dr. Bradley would turn to me. In all the years I have known Dr. Benjamin Bradley there was never, even a hint of scandal. Then Jane steps into his life and unkind rumors are spread about him. She was not good for him! Luanne never gave him any grief. Look what Jane has done!" She shook her finger wildly at Jane. "Dr. Bradley became the object of the worst kind of gossip. Never, before Jane, was there ever a bad word said about him! Not even a hint of gossip!"

"Miss Fields are you aware you have just confessed to the attempted murder of Dr. Jane Bradley?"

"Yes." She hissed again, I am only sorry she survived. At least I saved Dr. Bradley from having to deal with another child, and now she can never have any more babies! The deed is done!" She said in a gleeful, evil sounding tone.

It had taken a roundabout way with questions that seemed irrelevant but prosecutor Wraith had slammed the final and most important self incriminating trap shut with the help of some others in that courtroom.

The spectators were loud in their astonished exclamations. Looking over at Benjamin and Jane, Sergeant Liston noticed Jane appeared to look faint. He

229

and his partner rushed over to the couple and helped them out of the courtroom before the assembly of reporters could block their way.

Chapter 23 - Lasting Memories

Jane suddenly noticed some early activity on and around the Overlook High School football field. It wouldn't be long, she thought, before the start of the game. Soon her attention would need to be on the players of both teams, as the presiding physician for the game.

She got up from the bench to stretch her legs and took a few deep breaths. A glance at her watch told her she had been sitting for some time, and a little walk was in order.

As Jane walked, memories from that time in court, and immediately afterwards, came rushing back. Sergeant Liston drove them home in Ben's car, while Patrick Burton followed in the unmarked patrol car.

She remembered clearly how especially good it felt to be home. Even Ben noted how good it felt to be able to shut the door on a cold conspiring world.

Later, they would realize the spectators in the courtroom and those who read the newspapers account of the trial were very sympathetic to the Bradleys. Word soon got out that the Bradleys were seriously planning on leaving the area for good.

Editorials, letters to the editor, personal letters, all reflected the high regard the people in the surrounding areas held for the Bradleys. Still, it took several people to convince them to stay.

From then on the years flowed on the natural course of ups and downs for Ben and Jane. But with those ups and downs their love for each other grew. Benjamin felt richly blessed in all aspects of his life. His belief that God had saved the best for last for him never wavered.

It was a bright sunny afternoon Monday, May 28 when Ben and Jane walking arm in arm had finished their tour of the outer perimeter of the new Medical Research Center. "It will be some months, I think, before the inside will be ready for the scientists to settle in. That will be a very special day for me, Jane."

"I know, Ben, and you deserve all the accolades that will surely come to you.

"You've worked so long and hard and with great patience to bring to life the Research Center. I am so proud of you, Ben."

Benjamin smiled and pressed her arm against him in a warm, appreciative gesture. "Look, the stand of lilac trees are in bloom. Let's go sit on the bench in front of them," he suggested.

Once they were seated, Benjamin Franklin Bradley began to reminisce. "You know Jane, today with the sun shining and the lilacs blooming and us sitting on this bench, I am reminded of the day I handed you the acceptance letter from the Board. What a day and night that was!" He smiled as he asked, "Do you remember?"

Jane drew in a deep breath and let it out slowly before answering. "I could never forget that day; it was a beautiful beginning for us. I almost missed out on this life with you. If you hadn't looked for me and found me in the bus terminal and insisted I go back with you to your house…"

"I couldn't let you slip away because I was certain you were meant for me and I had to pursue what I believed. I consider myself to be a fortunate man to have a wife that gave me life's most precious Ls; love, laughter and loyalty. No man could ask for more from his wife."

"You remember Ben, I told you I would make it up to you when I said I couldn't afford a wedding band for you. Well, what better way than to give you love, laughter, loyalty, and with a little mystery mixed in, to make it up to you." Jane proffered her most endearing smile to Ben.

Ben circled Jane's waist with his arms and kissed her lovingly there on the bench beneath the fragrant lilac trees.

Chapter 24 - Twilight

Ben was at his desk in the Switzer General Hospital, Hospital Administrator's Office on Monday, January 17, 1983 when Jane stepped in and sat down in the plush chair immediately in front of his desk.

Smiling, she greeted Ben with, "Good morning sunshine. Why didn't you wake me up, birthday boy?" she asked in a teasing tone.

"You will not let me forget that sunshine greeting, will you?"

"Nope, and you will notice there is only you and me in this room, to hear it."

"Jane, be a good girl for me on my birthday, will you? Don't bring up negatives from our past," he simply asked.

"Okay, I won't, I'm sorry."

"Thank you," he smiled.

Sometimes when Ben smiled, Jane would see him as he was beyond the years that now marked his face, and as he looked when they met in 1958. At the moment, his face was as she remembered it. She got up walked around his desk and planted a long passionate kiss on his lips. "Happy Birthday, sweetheart."

Jane had taken a step back when Benjamin caught her hand, and stood up from his chair and then held her tight against him. "Jane, I will always love you with all my heart and soul."

In a barely audible voice Jane said, "I know Ben, and I ask that we may be blessed with many more years together here on earth."

Ben continued to hold Jane snug against him with both arms around her. "I ask God every day for more time. This old man doesn't want to leave you."

Jane and Ben were still in an embrace when Ben's office door suddenly swung open.

"Oops, are we interrupting?" they asked their parents as they separated themselves from each other.

"Not at the moment, you aren't," their father answered. "Come on in, boys, and take a seat."

"Happy Birthday, Dad," they said at the same time.

Before his father could reply, Scott spoke up. "We've been practicing singing happy birthday, like you used to for us. Would you like to hear us harmonize?"

"Ah, not right now boys. Later, thank you."

"So, the next pressing question is what would you like for your birthday, Dad?" Young Ben asked.

"From you two?" their father asked.

"Yup," they answered.

"Nothing that's going to cost me a lot of money," the senior Benjamin answered.

"Oh, come on Dad, what would you like?"

"What is it I might want, that you two could use?" Grinning, Benjamin asked, "Is that what you really want to know?"

"How about dinner for all of us?" Scott suggested.

"Good, I can afford that," Benjamin said.

"You can pick where we go to dinner, Dad," Scott Allen's smile broadened as he teased his father.

Laughing, Benjamin said, "Thank you Scott, I appreciate that option. Guess that's settled, we'll go out for dinner. A gift from my sons! You two are picking up the tab, right?"

"Yup," young Benjamin boldly answered, while Scott's eyes widened.

"It's times like this I miss the Van Durham. Do you remember the first time I took you there, Jane?"

"I certainly do. I had my favorite prime rib, and you wouldn't tell me how much it cost. It was an excellent dinner." Jane now turned to her sons. "By the way, boys, aren't you suppose to be doing something about your studies today?"

"It's Dad's birthday!" young Benjamin answered and added, "and our great grandfather's to the eleventh generation too. So, since we are related to two great men

234

we decided in honor of them, we should take the day off and celebrate."

"Now, did you?" their father asked as he walked around his desk so that he could address them at closer range. "Since I am one of the two great men you mentioned and I have to work and cannot take the day off, I strongly advise you two to hurry on over to where you are suppose to be and pay attention to your studies. The same ones I'm paying for! Tonight we can celebrate!"

Out in the hallway Scott said to Benjamin, "Where are we going to get the money to pay for dinner tonight?"

"Have you forgotten, Scott, we have a mother. She won't let us be embarrassed in public. She'll give us the money."

"One good thing about this," Scott began.

"What's that?" Benjamin asked.

"Apparently dad and mom haven't heard the Van Durham is going to reopen under the management of the original owner's grandson."

"When?"

"I don't know."

"Well, as long as it isn't tonight. In case we have to count our change to pay for dinner. You never know with Mom when it comes to money!"

"Yeah, but I'm banking on the fact she won't let us be embarrassed. She'll come through if she has to; after all this is for Dad," Young Benjamin suggested with confidence.

Benjamin Franklin Bradley's sons had not yet reached the exit door on the first floor when they heard code Red 711 on the hospital-wide paging system. Immediately the brothers turned around and ran to the nearest elevator and took it up to the seventh floor. When they arrived in their father's office it was empty; even Marsha his secretary was gone.

Leaving the office, the young Bradley men raced back to the elevators. They got off on the floor where recently an

Intensive Care Unit with its own ER had been created. This special section had been the brainchild of their father, intended in particular for heart attack emergencies. Their father had persuaded the Board at Overlook Memorial and their Hospital Administrator to establish a similar section in that hospital as well.

The double doors to the new emergency procedure room were wide open. Inside were several doctors, nurses, and technicians all working feverishly to save one life, Dr. Benjamin Franklin Bradley's life. To the side and out of the way was their mother. Marsha was standing beside her. Jane's face was pale and drawn as she watched the medical staff fight to save her husband's life.

Young Ben and Scott quickly took their places beside their mother. Marsha stepped apart as Young Ben placed his arm around his mother's shoulder while Scott held her hand. Moments later three clerics entered the room. All three were familiar faces in the hospital. Rabbi Cushman reached Jane first. He took her hand in his and saw with sorrow the tear-streak face slowly lift up and face him. "Jane," he spoke softly. "Don't lose hope. While there is breath there is hope."

Father Woods and Reverend Brook nodded their heads, agreeing with the Rabbi. Little was said as the Bradleys, the kindly clerics and Marsha waited, bound in silent prayer, for some encouraging word.

It was more than an hour later when Dr. Collins, a young cardiologist, addressed Jane and the group surrounding her. "He's stable now, we are going to bring him into a room here. We will be constantly monitoring him." Collins spoke in a cautious tone as he tried to convey optimism.

He was aware Jane was in shock and any details on Ben's condition would be lost on her right now. He took her hands in his and spoke softly. "He put up a good fight, and that's a good sign," he said as he smiled encouragingly.

She breathed out a long-held worried sigh as her mind registered what the doctor had just said and proffered a grateful smile.

Their two sons stepped aside as Ben was being wheeled out by two orderlies, followed by one of the nurses, while Dr. Collins spoke to Jane. Before Jane left the Intensive Care Unit ER, the three clerics promised to pray for Ben's recovery and visit the family. She thanked them, and with her sons beside her, they walked into the room next to this special ER where Ben was being made comfortable. Marsha returned to her office to handle the day's business in between the anticipated inquiring calls concerning Dr. Benjamin Bradley.

After everyone had left except his family, Ben said "Fortunately, God doesn't want me now. Otherwise I couldn't have put up the fight Collins spoke of."

"Ben you're remarkable, most people coming through what you have tend to be disoriented." Ben's alertness gave Jane hope. She was grateful for that.

"You know, Ben, Scott, I want to be around for your commencements. That means a lot to me," their father spoke purposely to his sons.

"So, you'll keep fighting Dad, won't you, for us, and Mom too?" There was a quiver in Scott's voice as he spoke.

"Promise us, Dad. You always keep your promises, Dad," Young Benjamin demanded.

"I'll do my best, boys," Benjamin said.

"Promise?" Young Ben asked.

"Yes Ben, I promise. Now I think you two need to go to class, and we'll all meet here tonight, dinner will be on me, here. Okay?" Ben proffered a weak but reassuring smile to his children.

"Are you sure, Dad?" Ben was certain he knew what his younger son, Scott was really asking and he knew his answer had to encourage both men.

"I'm sure," Benjamin said.

237

Both young men kissed their father on the top of his head as he always did with them. Before they left the room they kissed their mother on the cheek, and they each gave her a reassuring smile.

"We'll meet you here, Mom," Young Benjamin called out to his mother as he reached the doorway.

Jane nodded her head yes, and gave him a brave smile.

"Now Jane...," Benjamin began.

"You are not throwing me out, Benjamin Franklin Bradley!"

Ben smiled at his wife. "No, I'd like you to sit in this chair beside me, it looks more comfortable." He tried gesturing towards the chair but his arm dropped by his side.

"Rest, Ben, I'll be here, right beside you." Jane sat in the chair beside him, and took his hand and held it with tenderness.

At peace, and very grateful his life was preserved, Ben closed his eyes as he lay in his hospital bed quietly thinking about the future. His wife, his sons needed him, he knew. He did not want to leave them now. Benjamin began thinking about what patients had told him about beating the odds, living longer than expected, and surviving the deadliest of medical conditions.

Their bottom lines were prayer and attitude. It was Ben's attitude that moved him to fight to live. Even so, Benjamin was aware he had now entered the twilight time of his life.

Chapter 25 - Nightfall

"Someday each and every one of us will face the end of our earthly existence; when our twilight time begins, we sense our nightfall awaits us right around the bend."

Taking a deep saddened breath, Father Terrance Woods continued, "Benjamin Franklin Bradley was a doctor, husband, father and a true friend to many. He will be greatly missed by the many but especially by his family." Jane absently nodded her head in assent to Father Woods's words, as she sat in the first pew in St. Thomas' Roman Catholic Church in Glenwood.

Her sons Ben and Scott sat on either side of her. Josh and Lisa and their family filled up the rest of the pew. Behind them, across the aisle and in the loft above them, people from all walks of life packed the church. Benjamin had lived seven years after that first heart attack, and during the last half of those years he returned to his Catholic upbringing, the faith of his childhood. Jane always accompanied him whenever he attended church. Having her beside him, he said, was a comfort. At seventy-four Benjamin's mind was still sharp as ever. A few days before his death Ben told Jane he would escort her into Eternity when it was her time.

One Sunday in early spring, after attending mass, Benjamin drove them to the Ridge. He leaned across Jane as he had the first time he took her to the Ridge, and every time after that, and as always he opened the glove compartment and took the gate key out. But this time instead of getting out of the car and opening the gate he handed the key to Jane, something he had never done before.

"Jane, do you think you can unlock the gate?" he asked in his quiet voice.

Surprised, she answered, "I think so." Stepping out of the car, she unlocked the gate, and motioned for Ben to drive through. Once he drove safely past the gate Jane shut the gate and locked it, as Ben had always done, before getting back into the car.

Ben drove to the base of the Ridge and stopped the car. He looked up at the well-worn path as far as he could see and sadly shook his head. "I'm afraid the path up is too slick. I don't think we can make it up to the Ridge."

Jane reached over and patted his arm "That's all right, Ben, we'll come up here this summer," she said in an encouraging tone.

Without a word Benjamin turned the motor off as they looked at the path up the Ridge. Turning in his seat, Ben faced Jane. She saw there was deep sadness reflected in his eyes. Seeing his eyes like that, Jane's eyes grew moist.

Swallowing hard, Jane asked, "What is it Ben, what's the matter?"

"There are things, Jane, I want you to know just in case..."

"Oh, Ben please, what is it, I thought ...you told me Gallagher and Collins said you were doing fine." Ben heard the quivering in her soft voice. "Did you lie to me, Ben?"

No longer able to stand seeing the tears forming in her eyes, or listen to the quivering in her voice, Benjamin slid over to her and pulled her up to him. "I didn't lie to you Jane. But I have to tell you things you need to know, just in case. Please don't make it harder for me, Jane." Jane took a deep breath and slowly let it out. Ben felt the tension slowly slip out of her body.

"Jane, after my heart attack I realized I had to make some arrangements. Arrangements that I didn't want you to have to take care of. Our attorney, Jason, has everything in writing that will explain it all to you. But I have taken care of everything," he reassured her, without going into details, knowing the details would disturb her. "Most important to me is that you know I will still love you in Eternity," he said.

Jane could no longer hold back the tears. "Ben, I don't want you to leave me alone."

240

For a long time the two clung to each other. "I promise you Jane, when it's your time I'll come for you, you won't be alone." Jane's sobbing was muffled somewhat as she buried her face in Benjamin's broad shoulder.

After a while Jane started to gain control of herself and said, "But Ben, when you see her again, you'll probably forget your plain Jane," she cried.

"Who, Jane?"

"Your Luanne, she'll probably be even more beautiful in eternity then she was here on earth."

"Oh, for God's sake Jane!" Ben laughed. "After all these years and all that we have been to each other do you think I could be so shallow?" Ben suddenly became serious as he tipped her face up towards him. "Jane, I never loved her as much as I love you. I told you a long time ago there was no one between you and me. Not then, not now, not ever. Please believe me, Jane, for our sakes later on."

Jane pulled herself together as she leaned back in Ben's arms. "You know Ben, men can be very stupid when it comes to women."

Ben smiled broadly as he pulled her up even closer to him. "You don't have anything to worry about Jane, but I do have something to confess, so my conscience will be clear."

"What, Ben?" she asked with a worried look on her face.

"First, I don't know why I didn't tell you this years ago. Actually it was kind of a nonsense sort of thing. The truth is, Jane, I am the friend I told you who owned this land, including the Ridge."

Jane laughed. "Why, Ben..?"

"If I knew the answer to that, I'd be a genius! It was just one of those things you say and don't know why you said it. But I would like you to keep it forever wild. Don't sell this land." Smiling, he added, "I wouldn't want the angels flying on top of the Ridge to be displaced."

"Oh Ben, you are such a character!" she laughed. But then Jane became serious. She felt a certain urging she couldn't explain. "There is a secret I want to tell you, but you have to promise you will not repeat it to anyone, neither will you become angry about it."

"What is it, Jane?"

"You have to promise," she insisted.

Benjamin hesitated but then said, "I promise I won't repeat what you say or get angry."

Jane studied Benjamin as he spoke; he sounded and looked so strong and she was pleased. "I'm going to hold you to that promise, Ben.

"Apparently, there have been a number of people who have approached the Research Medical Center Board members and requested that the building be named after you. In fact, as I understand it, several people have promised large donations to the Research Building project if the building is named after you. I was asked what I thought of the idea, and I said it was a splendid idea."

"Jane, I don't want any recognition. I just thought a medical research center would be a boon for the town, the university, the hospital and all people..."

"Benjamin," she interrupted him, "I told the Board it would be a fine thing. So, don't you try and change anyone's mind; besides think of our sons."

"What do they have to do with this?"

"Imagine how nice it will be for them to see how much the people respect you and appreciate your work in this area. They will have to live up to their father's reputation, and that will be good for them and the patients they serve."

Benjamin did not offer any more of an argument. Since Jane knew him to be a medical man of true humility, she could only assume Ben was weaker than he would admit. He offered no more arguments and that worried her. That was the last time Benjamin and Jane went to the Ridge together.

Later that day, Benjamin was rushed to the hospital. At first, it seemed Ben had won the battle. Jane was at his side and saw the proud smile on his face, despite the pain he was feeling, when he heard over the hospital paging system: "Dr. Benjamin Franklin Bradley Junior, Dr. Scott Allen Bradley..." as the two young doctors were directed to the cardiac unit.

Jane's heart was breaking as she saw that there was little hope Ben would win this last battle for life. "Ben, I love you, please don't leave me," Jane pleaded as her tears flowed swiftly down her face.

"I love you Jane, no regrets, no regrets, I have no regrets..." Those were Dr. Benjamin Franklin Bradley's last words to his beloved, Jane.

Jane's mind returned to the present as Father Woods spoke on the readings of the 'Good Sheppard'. As she listened to his homily, her eyes went to the closed casket that rested in the center aisle near the first pew. She was still finding it hard to believe Benjamin Franklin Bradley was gone. And gone with him were the years worth living, she thought.

In the silence of her heart Jane called out, "Oh Ben, I truly love you, I love you big time, Ben. I hope you can hear me, wherever you are. You were the best that could have happened to me."

Following the funeral Mass, the limousine took Jane, her sons, her brother and his family to the Glenwood Cemetery on what seemed like a long way around the cemetery. Finally, the limousine came to a stop in a place that looked like a small cove. A mausoleum had been placed in between spreading lilac trees. In front of the mausoleum was a stone bench similar to the ones she and Ben had sat on in the days of their courtship in Chicago. It was the first thing Jane noticed. Then she looked long on the left side of the mausoleum, where Dr. Benjamin Franklin Bradley's name had been scripted in wrought iron

243

and below that were the dates of his birth and death. On the right side was "Dr. Jane Potts Bradley" scripted in wrought iron and the date she was born. Jane was deeply touched by the details Ben had arranged beforehand. Ben had in fact taken care of everything as he had said he would.

Jane sighed as she watched her husband's remains being placed in the mausoleum. Without thinking, Jane suddenly looked up to the very peak of Ben's final resting place and gasped. Carved in the stone was "Jane, my love for you is eternal. Ben." Below that was the date they were married, June 2, 1958.

It was later that year in the autumn when the Dr. Benjamin Franklin Bradley Medical Research Building was ready for the scientists and staff to move in. On Sunday afternoon, October 23, 1988, the dedication of the building was held before a large interested crowd.

Jane stepped into the building shortly after the conclusion of the speeches. Just as it was at the cemetery, Jane had not seen the mausoleum before Ben's interment, neither had Jane ventured inside the Research Building before that afternoon.

Escorted by her sons, Jane gasped and came to a complete stop a few feet into the center corridor. On the left hand side of the wide doorway into the main section of the building, behind a glass enclosure, was a life-sized portrait of Benjamin in his lab coat with a stethoscope around his neck holding a chart in his hands. It was made from a copy of a photograph taken years before, and one that Jane dearly loved. The portrait was so lifelike that it startled her. On the opposite side was another same size glass enclosure containing an open scroll detailing Benjamin's life, including his kinship to Benjamin Franklin.

On either side of the open foyer were long comfortable-looking padded benches.

With Young Ben and Scott beside her, Jane slowly walked over to the bench closest to Ben's portrait and sat down. "Mother, are you all right?" Young Ben asked as he bent towards her.

"Yes, Ben, I just need to catch my breath," she replied.

Scott moved closer to the tall glass display and studied the painting. When he turned around he said, "It's an excellent likeness of Dad. For a minute I thought Dad was..." He left the rest of what he was going to say slip away in silence as he saw the sadness in his mother's eyes on him.

Ben sat down next to his mother and took her hand in his. "Mom, do you want to go on?"

"I would rather not Benjamin, I am tired."

"Just rest for awhile, Mom," he lovingly suggested.

"Mom, there are four corridors that lead off from here. I'm sure you will not want to walk down them today, but I think you should know each corridor has a name. The first one is named Dr. Jane Bradley, the second Dr. Benjamin Franklin Bradley Junior; the third is Dr. Scott Alan Bradley and fourth is Dr. Alan Bradley." Scott stated.

"Oh, how nice," she exclaimed. "Did your father recommend the names for the corridors?"

"No, Mom he did not, the Board did."

"Your father would be pleased to see his father's name on one of the corridors. I'll send a thank-you note to the Board."

"Mom, there is a reception being held downstairs in the cafeteria..."

Jane sighed. "I feel so drained. I would like to go home. You two should stay and express my deepest gratitude again for honoring your father and for honoring you two boys, and his father. Oh, and me too, and make my excuses. Please, I really can't handle any more. I'll call a cab," she said as she tried to smile.

"No, Jane, I will drive you home. I was afraid this would be too much for you," he said.

245

The three Bradley's looked up. Standing nearby, like an unobserved guardian angel, was the tall broad-shouldered figure of a good friend.

Made in the USA
Charleston, SC
12 January 2013